CHINESE MUSICAL INSTRUMENTS

Chinese Music Monograph Series

ISSN: 1071-5649

Series Editors:
Yuan-Yuan Lee Ph.D.
Sin-yan Shen Ph.D.

- ■ CHINESE MUSIC AND ORCHESTRATION: *a Primer on Principles and Practice*

- ■ CHINESE MUSICAL INSTRUMENTS

- ■ CHINA: *A Journey into Its Musical Art*

- ■ WHAT MAKES CHINESE MUSIC CHINESE?

- ■ MUSICIANS OF CHINESE MUSIC

- ■ THE REGIONAL MUSIC OF CHINA

CHINESE MUSICAL INSTRUMENTS

Yuan-Yuan Lee
&
Sin-yan Shen

CHINESE MUSIC SOCIETY OF NORTH AMERICA
CHICAGO   USA

CHINESE MUSICAL INSTRUMENTS
Copyright © Chinese Music Society of North America, Chicago, USA, 1999
First Edition, 1999
First Printing, 1999

Published in the United States of America by the Chinese Music Society of North America, One Heritage Plaza, P.O. Box 5275, Woodridge IL 60517-0275 USA. http://ChineseMusic.Net

Library of Congress Catalog Card Number 99-75864

Library of Congress Cataloging in Publication Data
Lee, Yuan-Yuan
              Chinese Musical Instruments (Chinese Music Monograph Series)
              ISBN 1-880464-03-9
              1. Music--China--History and criticism.   2. Musical instruments--China.
              3. Orchestra.   4. Composition.   5. Acoustics.   6. Performance. I.
              Shen, Sin-yan, 1949- II. Series
ML336.L385 1999
784'.0951--dc20
Total 208 pages
140 Illustrations
Bibliographical references and Index

Chinese Music Monograph Series books, the Chinese Music international journal, music full scores, sheet music, instrumental instruction books, recordings and other educational material are available from the Chinese Music Society of North America, National Headquarters, P.O. Box 5275, Woodridge IL 60517-0275 USA. Tel: 630-910-1551   FAX: 630-910-1561   http://ChineseMusic.Net

Chinese Musical Instruments

■ CONTENTS

■

Chinese Musical Instruments

■

AUTHORS' NOTE

Material for this book has been developed over the years teaching at the graduate and the undergraduate levels and at the Research Institute of the Chinese Music Society of North America. Extensive material is also drawn from our masterclasses at music festivals, music schools and music departments all through North America and internationally during our concert tours.

Pursuing our exploration of the almost limitless caverns of Chinese music and orchestration, so much of which has never yet come to the knowledge of the rest of the world, we approach the subject from both the angles of principles and practice. Functional discussions of musical interest, cultural molding of musical psychology, instrumental effects and acoustics are emphasized. The exploration centers on the principle of cultural acoustics, that is the impacts of musical acoustics is strongly modified by our ear and brain which are products of culture.

The intended audience are students of music at the university level, and music practitioners. The book is written so that it requires no prior knowledge of Chinese music or acoustics. Also, no knowledge of the Chinese language is assumed.

With the opening chapter we find ourselves at a focal point in the present study: The Cultural Acoustics of Chinese Musical Instruments? The cultural preference of harmony, and thus intervals and tones and rhythms used in music, distinguishes one music from another. Chinese music, however,

Chinese Musical Instruments

is unique in its uninterrupted history of more than 8000 years and very early development of theoretical systematics, acoustical and material science, and orchestral practice.

The bronze bell chime is perhaps the ultimate percussion instrument. The world's first double reed instrument, the guanzi, is really not a double reed using present day nomenclature. The qin is timeless in the true sense of the word. The Chinese orchestra is several dozens of acoustically unified and musically interesting orchestras, primarily based on reeded wind and plucked strings as orchestral tone quality bases. The principal instrumental subgroups of reeded wind, plucked string, and bowed string are then studied in detail in succeeding chapters. The orchestral roles, acoustics, performance practice, orchestration techniques and repertoire of each group form the key areas of discussion. Numerous practical examples are used throughout to aid the discussion.

It is with the greatest pleasure that we thank the great many members of our audience on our North America and international tours who constantly suggested that we wrote this book. Colleagues in theory, composition, and performance throughout the world had stimulated the completion of this text. The masters of Chinese music and acoustical masters throughout the ages inspired our theoretical and practical approach.

We specially thank our parents for without their constant encouragements and guidance over the years this work would not have been possible, and without the open-minded cultural environment provided by them in our youth the subject of cultural acoustics would not have appeared.

■

The Cultural Acoustics of Chinese Musical Instruments

Years ago while we were still developing the field of Cultural Acoustics, many colleagues asked me "I've been playing the *erhu* for a while now - how come I still can't get the proper tone - It just doesn't sound Chinese!". There the connection between tone and cultural acoustics is but one aspect of the problem. The music of China is built on a specific harmonic system, and that harmonic system is not only different but also broader than what is known in the West, especially when the current prevalence of the equal-tempered scale system is included. Chinese music came from natural and physically just intervals. That is why Chinese string tuning is stacked fifth-fourth in all respects rather than the fifth-fifth stacking as is practiced in the West today, and exemplified by the violin family, which includes the violin, the viola, and the cello. The primary difference between musical systems of different culture is their preference for intervals, and thus a difference in the breadth of their harmonic system. Let me now explain the meaning of the breadth of one's harmonic system. In all compositions, there are intentional conflicts between harmony and discord. But what is harmonic and what is not is extremely

culture-specific. In present-day European and American music
the second is a discord while it is not in China. Here we are
dealing with specific intervals, but in reality it always is the total
combined effect of many intervals, while your brain still
remembers them, whether they be sounding at the same time or
slightly apart, that causes your brain to be stimulated in desired
fashion. In the performance of a single instrument, such
harmonic stimulation comes into play in the interaction between
the player and the instrument - thus his or her tone. Frequently
musicians do not think of the tone as a harmonic entity but it
absolutely is. The cultural acoustical preferences of a race or a
nationality determines the types of tone of instruments it accepts.
This explains why certain instruments sound Chinese, whether
you are familiar with it or not. However, with a Chinese
instrument, the way you play it can still make it sound utterly
blend and thus not Chinese - one example is to ask a violin
player to play the *erhu*. Without becoming accustomed to the
acoustical resonances of the *erhu*, the violin player may think it
is just another string instrument on which you are to divide the
strings. The *erhu* and the violin are wildly different instruments
in that the performance of the *erhu* actually requires the
production of acoustics that maximizes the contrast between its
major resonance components, whereas the philosophy behind the
development of the violin was even out register differences as
much as possible.

Chinese music is built on a totally consistent harmonic
system which controls melodic progression, orchestration, and
temperament use. It is perhaps the only major musical system in

the world that has such all-encompassing requirements on all aspects of its music, and at the same time allowing the largest flexibility in the acceptance of harmonic intervals into music. In the 1960s and the early 1970s through the work of the Chinese Music Society of North America, we discovered the cyclical harmonic skeletons known as *zhi, shang, yu, jue, gong* in the Chinese harmonic system. Before this work, those terms were for a long time referred to as scale steps. This set of harmonis skeletons is self generating, always in tune without equalizing temperaments because its system does not believe in the twelve tones alone. The same harmonic intervals which are the basis of the Chinese harmonic system were found to appear prominently in the design of the overtone structure of the ancient dual-pitched bronze *zhong* bells (see Shen, 1987). The same harmonic intervals are completely utilized in the design of Chinese silk and bamboo musical instruments, and in particular, is the basis for string tuning on the *qin*, the *sanxian*, the *zheng*, the *pipa*, the *erhu*, the *tuoyin erhu*, the *matouqin*, the *zhuihu*, the *jinghu*, the *banhu*, the *liuqin*, and the *ruan* family. This I believe I first discussed in 1976 at the First Chinese Music International Conference held at Northwestern University in Chicago. It, however, was not until the discovery of the Zenghou Yi bell chime in 1978 that furthered my understanding of the relationship between the overtone structure of musical instruments selected by a certain musical system and the harmonic preferences of the system. In retrospect it should have been obvious that this was the case. As soon as the Zenghou Yi bells were discovered, We immediately lauched a massive project looking into the acoustics of ancient Chinese bronze bells. In that project we were able to, in great detail, separate the musical bells from the non-musical bells. We studied complete overtone structure of all existing Shang and Zhou bells and was delighted to find the acousitcal design of bells of each period, and in particular in the case of the *zhong* musical bells established direct connection between the choice of their overtone structure and the Chinese harmonic system as we know it today. Acoustics is thus a cultural thing, in addition to being a physical thing!

REFERENCES

Shen, Sinyan, Acoustics of Ancient Chinese Bells, *Scientific American*, **256**, 94 (1987).

Shen, Sin-yan, *Chinese Music and Orchestration: A Primer on Principles and Practice*, Chinese Music Society of North America, Chicago (1991).

■

Historical Trends in Preferences for Musical Instruments

The system of Chinese musical instruments is a family of musical instruments utilizing all available acoustical material and resonators. In fact the name reserved for musical instruments is "qin'", or resonator. The history of Chinese musical instruments has been a history of new resonator discovery, new use of physiology in acoustical excitation, and musical acoustics. Acoustical research in the 20th Century revealed a most distinguished history of the science of music in China. Ancient China possessed a level of acoustical science that was essential in supporting the elaborate musical art of those periods. Physics and engineering worked hand in hand to perfect musical instruments and to arrive at desirable orchestration. Coupled acoustical systems were invented in every period. New performing methods

---

'Today the name *qin* refers to the seven-string zither without bridge. But in the minds of the Chinese, *qin* simply means musical instrument, e.g. in "lian qin le mei you?" (Have you practiced your musical instrument today?). The Chinese name of the violin is named after a Chinese bowed string popular in Kunqu Opera call the "*tiqin*" (which literally means a *qin* that you carry). The violin is shorter than the tiqin, thus it is called "*xiao tiqin*" (a small *tiqin*) to indicate that it is a small bowed string.

were found in all regions. Throughout the ages preference for musical instruments have changed greatly. Very early instruments naturally emphasized wind and percussion. Globular flutes *xun* and end-blown flutes *xiao*[2] first appeared in China 8,000 years ago. Panpipes *yue* and mouthorgans *he* were invented very early. The early invention of silk strings formed the basis of the design of string instruments. The bronze age brought about the fabulous dual-pitched Chinese musical bells.

SHANG-ZHOU: COMPLETION OF ALL INSTRUMENTAL GROUPS

During the early dynasties of the Shang (16th-11th Century BC) and Zhou (16th Century-221 BC) period, sophisticated stringed musical instruments were used which were not to be carried when played (unlike the later lutes and fiddles which are portable) and they were all quite large - these were the times of *qin, se, zheng,* and the horizontal *konghou*[3]. These major instruments remain today, with the *se* becoming completely

---

[2] The oldest known vertical flutes were the *gudi,* the bone flutes. The oldest group of end-blown *gudi* is 8,000 years old found in Neolithic sites at Jiahu in Wuyang County of Henan (See Shen, 1991), and these Wuyang *gudi* contained the complete interval preferences of the Chinese people. But today *xiao* is the name given to end-blown flutes.

[3] The *konghou* is the harp. Old *konghou*s were horizontal, like the *qin,* and the *se.* The more popular *konghou* is vertical, and it became popular in the Han period. The konghou is used today as an accompaniment and orchestral instrument.

unpopular[4] nowadays. At a later time the bowed *yazheng* appeared to become popular, especially in Sui times. The *qin* utilized contrasts between harmonics, stopped strings, and open strings as major categories of tone quality in composition. The *se* was frequently used in *qin* and *se* duets - thus a fingerboard instrument is contrasted and supported by a bridged instrument. These instruments and the *zheng* were plucked, and the *yazheng* bowed. The resonator used here can be classified as a long box which amplifies notes made on strings which transmit their energy via ridges, posts or bridges. The one instrument which is uncommon after those periods was the *zhu*, on which a stick-bow was bounced on strings. On arts depicting *zhu* performance, e.g. in the Mawangdui relics, the *zhu* was played like a cello with the bow bouncing on its strings. The discovery of the musical treasure of Zenghou Yi from the 5th Century BC provided examples of two orchestras: one based on jin-shi-si-zhu (metal-stone-silk-bamboo) and another based on si-zhu (silk & bamboo). The large court orchestra was rather dynamic in volume and symphonic in acoustical impact, utilizing a large bell chime (a single musical bell is a *zhong* and a bell chime is called a *bianzhong*) which would occupy the complete stage of a chamber music recital hall today, and a large stone chime (a single musical

---

[4]The *se* is a bass string instrument. It works extremely well with the *qin* in a duet, and as bass instrument in an orchestra. The se is traditionally divided into two parts - top and bottom - when played, thus utilizing both hands in contrapuntal melodies at the same time. The *se* is still one of the best bass instruments for the Chinese orchestra, except because of the modern love for bowed strings it's been shelved.

stone is a *qing,* and a stone chime is a *bianqing).* This large orchestra utilized various mouthorgans in the categories of *yu* and *sheng* (the *yu* is a melodic instrument and the *sheng* is a harmonizing instrument, both in the free-reed mouthorgan category), the *yue* (panpipe) and the *chi* (the *chi* and the *di* are side-blown flutes[5]) and a large number of silk instruments such as the ones we already described above. There were the "Shi" Music Officers assigned to various lead instruments including the *zhong,* the *qing,* the *sheng,* the *yue,* the *bo* (ceremonial bell) and other musical instruments.

QIN-HAN PORTABLE LUTES

The next period of expansion in Chinese instrumental music was the Qin (221-207 BC) and the Han (206 BC-220 AD) period. During the Qin-Han period, many hand-carried and portable instruments became widely poplar. These included the *ruan, pipa, qinhanzi, hulei,* and others, which can best be classified in the lute family - but because of their performing technique, they really were vertical members of the "tantiao" family of China (see Shen, 1981 and Shen, 1991), the horizontal members of this family being the *qin,* the *zheng,* the *se* and the *yangqin.* One form or another of all of these instruments are in use today - thus this period is extremely important for Chinese instruments. Today three general groups of the vertical tantiao family are popularly known: (A) the *sanxian* group which uses

---

[5]Most ancient cultures had a number of end-blown flutes. China was the inventor of the side-blown flute, or transverse flute.

drum resonators covered with skin membrane on two sides, coupled to a fingerboard neck. Members include the large *sanxian* and the small *sanxian*, (B) the *ruan* group which uses disc-like resonator coupled to fretted neck. Members include the *ruan*, the *yueqin*, and the *qinqin*, and (C) the *pipa* group which uses pear-shaped resonator with convex back, with frets. Members include the *pipa*, and the *liuqin*.

WEI-JIN THROUGH TANG: REED & PERCUSSION AND FIDDLES

The Wei (220-265) and Jin (265-420) periods up to Tang (618-907) saw the complete disappearance of the bell chimes and the stone chimes. In fact, the dual-pitch design of the musical bells and the performance techniques were completely lost until the 20th Century[6]. Many portable percussion instruments were popular. These include the *bo* cymbal, the *paiban* for keeping tempo and orchestral direction. The *fangxiang* xylophone[7] was popular and completely replaced bell chimes and stone chimes.

---

[6]In 1978, after the Zenghou Yi musical treasures were unearthed, the Chinese Music Society of North America launched a comprehensive project on the study of the acoustics and performing techniques of the bianzhong, as part of our ongoing Chinese Harmony Project which looks into interval building blocks, temperaments, overtones of instruments, tuning of instruments, performance art of instruments, and composition and orchestration as one unified subject. During this project, the mystery regarding the design of the dual-pitch system on the zhong and the performing methods of the bianzhong was completely solved.

[7]At a later time, the *fangxiang* xylophone would be almost completely replaced by the *yunluo* gong chime, which is still popular in the 20th Century.

Chinese Musical Instruments

The Sui-Tang period fancied the use of double reeds. In particular the cylindrical double-reeded *bili* became a popular sound, together with the *jiegu* drum performed with two sticks. The famous Xuanzong Emperor of Tang composed several dozen musical numbers featuring the *jiegu* as solo instrument and the whole musical scene became very exciting with the popularity of various double reeds and percussion instruments from western China. The Sui-Tang courts were one of the biggest on number of musical staff. There were permanent installations of orchestras from more than ten different regions of China in the Tang courts. In addition to the *bili* as a double reed, the conical *suona* was popular. Also during the Sui-Tang period the age of true fiddling began. This was a time when bowed strings were officially imperial instrument. The Chinese fiddles are true fiddles in that they were intended to be bowed when invented and not converted from lutes. The *xiqin* fiddle of the Sui-Tang period, which used a long bamboo stick as its bow with no horsehair, became the predecessor of the present-day *banhu* fiddle. Then during the time of Genghis Khan various types of the Mongolian *matouqin* horse-head fiddle became known more widely to the majority of the non-Mongolian Chinese. This fiddle utilized a horse-haired bow. A cross-fertilization of fiddles then took place all across China and its vicinities. From this point on all fiddle players of China became exposed to bows with horse hair, and utilized it until the present time. This practice also influenced lute players and instrument makers in Europe who adopted the concept of the horse-haired bow for bowed lutes that would be used as new string instruments.

SONG TO THE PRESENT: FIDDLE POPULARITY

The Song (960-1279), the Yuan (1271-1368), the Ming (1368-1644) and the Qing (1644-1911) periods saw the consistent popularity of the fingerboard lute *sanxian,* which had been important in theatrical music and ballad singing during this time. In the Ming period, the great musician Wei Liangfu was a master of the fiddle *tiqin.* He used this fiddle as a main accompanying instrument for Kunqu singing and in the silk and bamboo ensemble. Compared with the *xiansuo* string music of the north, according to Li Yu of the Qing period, the *tiqin* was more crisp in tone. It's a long fiddle that used no *qianjin* (Thus the whole length of the strings were used) and bowed with horse-haired bow. The *tiqin* was popular before the *huqin,* and was later replaced by the *huqin.* Of course, the *huqin* family remain extremely popular today. Thus from Sui-Tang to the present time, we saw several developments pertaining to the fingerboard that are prevalent: (1) the popularity of plucked instruments with no frets, as well as (2) the popularity of bowed fiddles with and without a fingerboard[8]. Very few new resonators were introduced after the Sui-Tang period. The last dynasty-the Qing period was a time when the Qing court was very interested in reviving ancient instruments such as the *bianzhong* to ascertain a main-stream Chinese status. However, the Qing court failed

---

[8]The more regional *zhuihu, zhuiqin, leiqin* fiddles all use fingerboards, whereas the highly popular *erhu, zhonghu, banhu, jinghu* fiddles use stopped free strings with no fingerboard - a drastically different concept when it comes to left hand performance techniques, compared with fingerboard instruments.

21

miserably - they were able to construct only modest-quality ceremonial bells but not musical bells at all. As a result, many scholars in China and abroad during the Qing and the Republic period were also terribly confused about what was a *bianzhong* or how it was played. It showed a serious lack of understanding of Chinese musical culture during Qing times.

The 20th Century saw the elevation of many ensemble and orchestral instruments to a solo status. In particular, the second fiddle, already popular in its orchestral role because of the statistics of use in regional ensembles and orchestras, became the most popular solo instrument in ensemble and orchestral works. A disheartening phenomenon in the 20th Century is the collapse of the motive forces behind regional instrumental practices, as a handful "professional" composers try to simplify the orchestral scene in larger cities. They composed for a simplified Chinese orchestra which lost all of the musical interests and cultural acoustics of Chinese orchestras. They lost track of Chinese aesthetics, and most importantly, they lost track of the principles behind the acoustical space of the Chinese orchestra. Thus it is a matter of education, and a matter of the mind set.

The regions and provinces of China are drastically different culturally. The cultural acoustics of the music in each of them are individually unique, and yet all Chinese. The reason is that the Chinese were different peoples. The culture of the people are so different that a person from a neighboring province may or may not understand what he hears in this province. Over the thousands of years the Chinese people is unified by a single language and a single Harmony System. As a result we have the most interesting situation of the coexistence of many Chinese orchestras, each having its cultural acoustical specialties, and yet all unified by the Chinese Harmony System. It is thus a mistake to take apart the regional Chinese orchestras and try to produce a single Chinese orchestra, because they are already unified through the Harmony System. But it is highly desirable to broadly present the different ways of doing things instrumentally in these different regions and provinces, so that their cultural acoustics and musical interests can be further propagated and, most importantly, utilized in new compositions.

REFERENCES

Shen, Sin-yan, The Tantiao (Pipa) Strings, *Chinese Music,* **4**/1, 3 (1981).

Shen, Sinyan, Acoustics of Ancient Chinese Bells, *Scientific American,* **256**, 94 (1987).

Shen, Sin-yan, *Chinese Music and Orchestration: A Primer on Principles and Practice,* Chinese Music Society of North America, Chicago (1991).

∎

Musical Bells and Bell Chimes

Bronze bell chimes were important orchestral instruments until they vanished from history 2,000 years ago. A chime recovered by archaeologists has revealed their sophisticated acoustical design. In the 1970s and the early 1980s, we determined the theoretical design of the complete chimes, and connected their overtone structure to the Chinese harmonic system.

MUSICAL BELLS AND CEREMONIAL BELLS

To do our comprehensive survey of Chinese musical instruments, we must put the scale of development of these instruments in perspective - in that respect the musical bell chimes of China must be first introduced. The bell chimes were the largest musical instruments in their heyday. The bell chime was often complimented with a jade chime, or a stone chime for tonal contrast. Since there still is often a confusion outside China regarding what is a musical bell chime, let us first distinguish between the basic types of bells. Chinese ceremonial bells are called *bo*, and musical bells are called *zhong*. The *zhong* bells are used in large and small sets for performance of ensemble music and orchestral music. The Zenghou Yi *bianzhong* has the range of a Mozart piano, but is much more complete in truly just intervals. It offers the <u>closest design</u> to the Chinese 23 temperament system which is in active use all through the major part of history and today in Chinese music. The *zhong* bells are dual-pitched, and the *bo* bells are not[1]. We found that the *zhong* bells were designed to be dual-pitched so that more tones could be performed on each chime, and the attenuations of sound for each tone were designed to be high so that the *bianzhong* bell chime accommodate performance of rapid melodic movements.

ACOUSTICS OF ANCIENT CHINESE BELLS

In 1978, a set of Chinese bronze chime bells large enough to occupy the entire stage of a modern recital hall was unearthed in Hubei Province in southern China. The chime, which dates from the 5th Century BC, consists of 65 bells encompassing five octaves, a range greater than that of most contemporary instruments. A filigree of gold-inlaid inscriptions on the bells and their frame documents the existence of an elaborate theory of music that specified the design, scales and instrumentation of ancient orchestras. This record and recent investigations of the chime itself have prompted a complete rewriting of the history of acoustics.

---

[1]A number of major museums in the world still label their collection of *bo* bells as dual-pitched <u>by mistake</u>. This problem is however gradually being corrected now. For clarifications between the *zhong* and the *bo* and their proper definitions, see my paper in the *Scientific American* (Shen, 1987).

Chinese Musical Instruments

The ancient inscriptions confirms what modern scholars were only beginning to suspect: that the bells were constructed in such a way that each could produce two separate pitches. This property sets the Chinese chime bells apart from Western church bells, which are known for their single, lingering tones; unlike church bells, the chime bells could perform complex, rapidly metered music. For reasons that are not clear, the principles and practices surrounding the unique bell design were never passed down. Consequently, the way to play chime bells remained a mystery for more that 2,000 years.

The bells incorporate many unusual features whose sophistication and precision can be appreciated only in the light of the dual-pitch design. Since the chime was discovered, studies of vibrational properties and tuning methods have revealed the depth of understanding possessed by Chinese metallurgists and musicians. The design of the bells requires a theoretical grasp of physics and engineering formerly thought to have evolved only in the late 18th century. Indeed, the acoustical principles exploited in the Chinese bronze bells have astonished even 20th-century acousticians.

The study of acoustics in the Western world is relatively young. In 1781, a German physicist named Ernst F. Chladni sprinkled sand on vibrating plates to show that some regions of the plates remained stationary during vibration. These motionless regions were termed nodal lines; their distribution describes the modes a vibrating body assumes. Each so-called normal mode is associated with a characteristic frequency of vibration, and the frequency of vibration determines the perceived pitch.

Musical Bells & Bell Chimes

Vibrating bodies move in may different modes simultaneously and generate many different frequency components called partial. The partial with the lowest frequency is called the fundamental; there are many higher frequencies called overtones. When a bell is struck or a string is plucked, all these frequencies come into play, but some are stronger (louder) than others. The relative strength of partial in a musical sound constitutes its tonal quality, just as a combination of wavelengths determines the color of light.

In 1890, Lord Rayleigh studied the bells in the tower of his church in Terling, England, and performed experiments on several bells in his laboratory. He identified six partial in the bells. Rayleigh, who laid the foundation for subsequent work on bell acoustics, thought that a bell could produce just one fundamental pitch. Since his experience was confined to Western bells, he could not have foreseen the lesson that Chinese bells thousands of years old would teach.

About 80 years ago, single chime bells began to appear among other archaeological finds in China. Later sets and entire ensembles of the bells turned up; today thousands of bells and more than 50 chimes have been recovered. Although the bells were thoroughly scrutinized, instigators did not recognize the dual-pitch potential until 1977. Some doubts persisted until the 1978 discovery of the chime in Hubei Province.

There were earlier clues that had escaped notice. While studying the Jing-li bell chime, which had been unearthed in Henan Province in 1957, investigators at the National Music Research Institute played "The East Is Red" using pitches obtained by striking the bells at their center. An $^{\#}E_5$ was missing. Anxious to complete the piece, the team found the note by striking a $^{\#}C_5$ bell on its side. Their success was regarded as accidental.

In 1977, Huang Xiang-peng, Lu Ji, Wang Xiang, Gu Bo-bao and their colleagues at the institute examine a bell chime discovered in Shanxi Province and found that every bell, when struck on a side, produced a pitch higher that the one sounded from the center. The interval between the pitches was always a minor or major third, a difference in frequency equivalent to that between four or five consecutive keys on a piano. The team's observation sparked animated discussions about whether the phenomenon was accidental or deliberated, and whether the second pitch was a fundamental or an overtone.

The investigators than studied more than 200 bells from the Shang (16th to 11th Centuries BC) and Zhou (11th Century to 221 BC) periods, spanning the historical lifetime of the chimes. They concluded that the bells were deliberately constructed to produce two pitches. In one chime the side striking positions were decorated with glyphs of the phoenix, a practice presumably linked to ancient legends in which the singing of the phoenix connotes music.

When, a year later, the magnificent 65-bell chime was found in Hubei Province, the researcher's conclusion was borne out. The chime had been interred in the tomb of Zenghou Yi, marquis of an ancient principality known as Zeng. It was part of two large orchestras also preserved in the marquis's tomb. The bronze *zhong* bells, which combined make up a type of chime called *bian-zhong*, were intact and almost perfectly tuned. The

BELL CHIME of Zenghou Yi, ruler of a fifth-Century BC Chinese principality, is the most impressive set of *zhong* bells found to date. The chime consists of three tiers of bells mounted on a L-shaped frame. Exhaustive acoustical studies have shown how unique structural features enable each bell to sound two pristine fundamental pitches.

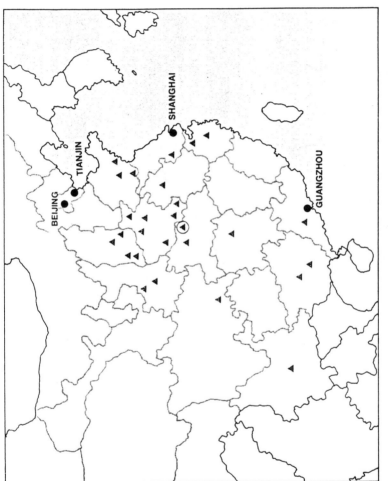

MAP OF BELL-CHIME DISCOVERY in China includes only the eastern and southwestern provinces because all the chimes were found there. More than 50 sets of bells have been unearthed since 1900. A circle marks the origin of Zenghou Yi's collection.

musical treasures of Marquis Yi confirmed the dual-pitch design of chime bells through detailed records inscribed on the bells themselves.

Because chime bells are intended to perform music in the company of orchestras, their desirable qualities are somewhat different from those of a ceremonial bell or a church bell. Each member of the chime should have a broad dynamic range and to allow the performance of complex melodies, its tones must please the ear and attenuate quickly, without a prolonged echo.

The geometric configuration of the chime bells is crucial to their achieving these acoustical properties. The *zhong* bell has an asymmetric construction. Unlike the church bell, which is circular in cross section, a *zhong* bell is oblate: its horizontal cross section is a flattened oval. The lip of the bell does not lie on a plane but arches upward in the front and back, then downward into hornlike feet on the left and right sides. The front and back faces meet at a ridge called the *xian*. Covering four regions of the upper bell body are 36 bronze nipples known as *mei*.

In a *bian-zhong* chime each *zhong* bell is suspended by a collar called the *xuan* from a hook mounted on the beam of the chime frame. The clapperless bells are arranged in tiers and played with different kinds of strikers. Usually bells of the high and middle registers are hung at or above eye level; the performers use hammerlike mallets. Bells of the low register are hung in the bottom row and are played using rods wielded in a near-horizontal trajectory.

A bell chime consisting of several dozen bells requires from five to seven performers. Performers of different registers stand on opposite sides of the chime. The bell mouth hangs downward at an angle of about 30 degrees from the vertical, balanced by a long, heavy nose called a *yong* that tilts toward the back so that the side to be played faces the performer. Depending on their pitch, the *zhong* bells range from a few inches to several feet in height: these last are relatively large instruments by modern standards.

The two fundamental pitches that give the bells their notoriety arise from tow distinct regions on the bell face. One pitch comes from the lower center of the bell, a position called *sui*, and the other from the areas to the left and right of the *sui*, and the other from the areas to the left and right of the *sui*, called the *gu* positions. The term *sui* is said to mean "mirror" and probably refers to the similarity between the curve of the lip and the concave burning mirror used at the time to start fires. *Gu* means "drum" or "music-producing." Because of a strong cultural emphasis on right-handedness, the right *gu* was played much more often than the left.

When played in a set, dual-pitch bells allow efficient performance and reduce the overall size of the bell chime. The design of Western bells is not nearly as practical. The "strike" tone of a western round bell (the pitch heard by a listener) is not the "hum," or fundamental tone, but the note an octave above the hum tone. For instance, a modern American bell with a fundamental pitch of middle C (C_4 at 256 cycles per second) has a perceived pitch of C_5 (512 cycles per second). It weighs 800

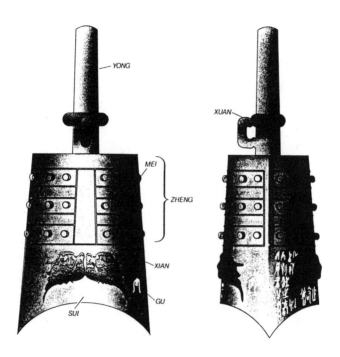

ZHONG BELL FEATURES are intimately related to the tonal quality and performance of the bell, shown here in front *(left)* and side views. The bell can produce two pitches because its cross section is asymmetrical; the tones are refined by bronze *mei* nipples. Some bells also carry inscriptions that indicate exact striking positions for each pitch.

pounds. According to the approximate rule that the pitch of the round bell is inversely proportional to the cubic root of its mass, a decrease in frequency by a factor of two would require eight times the original mass. An American bell with a middle-C strike tone would, therefore, weigh more than three tons--nearly 1,000 pounds more than all the bells and racks in the Zenghou Yi chime combined.

33

The inability to produce a bell that can sound its acoustical fundamental, then, has had serious implications for the material requirements and casting constraints of bell manufacture. Yet the church-bell design is the result of centuries of careful experimentation. The Chinese design, the result of thousands of years of labor, was lost after the Han period (206 BC to AD 220). What acoustical secrets does it embody that eluded Western designers?

A bell is very complex acoustical body. Its partial cannot be expressed as simple arithmetic ratios, in contrast to the completely elastic string or a vibrating air column whose frequencies correspond to the ratio 1:2:3:4:5:6 and so on. Both the oblate *zhong* bell and the round church bell are special adaptations of the acoustical system known as vibrating plates. For plates and bells alike, increasing the thickness and elasticity of the vibrating material increases diameter and density decreases the vibration frequency.

Mary D. Waller of the London School of Medicine for Women studied the normal modes of vibrating circular plates and published her results in 1937. Her nodal figures consist basically of radii (designated m) distributed symmetrically around the plate's center, and circles (designated n) concentric with the perimeter of the plate. The simplest mode, the one corresponding to the fundamental tone, exhibits four nodal lines that divide the plate into four vibrating sections shaped like pieces of pie. Adjacent segments are always moving in opposite directions at any given instant. The next mode, which generates a frequency 1.7 times that of the fundamental, has only one nodal circle, which delineates an inner circular segment and an outer ring. Other modes arise from additional combinations of radii and circles, creating a rich interplay of partial frequencies.

Acoustically, a round bell behave like a plate stretched into a flared bell shape and suspended at the center. The normal modes of a round bell, viewed from above, are quite similar to the patterns seen on circular plates. Vibrational motion is most intense at the rim. When the bell is given a blow, the struck side is forced inward and adjacent regions are pushed outward. The rim then passes through its initial circular shape to form another elongated circle at a right angle to the first.

In the course of these vibrations certain parts of the bell remain relatively still compared with others, namely the points at which the different circular distortions intersect. These points represent the nodal lines of the bell, called nodal meridians. They are not nodes in the strict sense, however, because the intersections are not exact, and so some motion continues to occur in the plane of the surface. This motion is what makes a glass goblet ring when one rubs a wet finger around the rim.

Nodal meridians on a round bell are spaced evenly, as are the nodal radii of a plate. Because of this symmetry, a clapper can be used with a round bell, since striking any point on the rim produces the same vibrational effects. The meridians of the asymmetrical *zhong* bell, on the other hand, are not evenly distributed. The consequence of this asymmetry is that, for any given number of nodal lines, more than one spatial arrangement is possible.

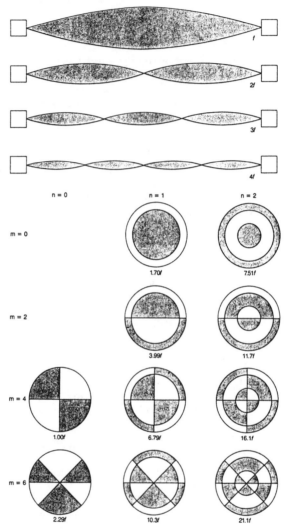

PARTIAL FREQUENCIES, which make up the tonal quality of a sound, result from the different modes of a vibrating body. The lowest frequency is called the fundamental; other frequencies are overtones. When a taut string is plucked *(top)*, it produces partial that are whole-number multiples of the fundamental frequency f. A vibrating plate *(bottom)*, however, gives rise to partial that cannot be related by simple arithmetic ratio. Instead frequencies depend on the combination of nodal radii *(m)* and nodal circles *(n)*, regions of the plate that remain still during vibration. Red and white represent movement in opposite directions. A bell, whether it is round or oblate, is a special kind of vibrating plate.

Indeed, the *zhong* bell has two well-defined sets of modes that can be selectively activated by striking different positions on the bell: the *sui* and *gu* positions. Although at the two fundamental pitches the modes have the same number of nodal lines ($m = 4$ and $n = 0$), the placement of the lines is indeed different, so that the frequencies generated are different. This "degeneracy" of vibrational modes accounts for the chime bells' extraordinary acoustical properties. In general, the *gu* mode produces higher frequencies that the *sui* mode, but the two are not mutually exclusive: they share certain high-frequency partial that issue from the more complex modes.

The ancient Chinese refined their dual-pitch design to make the two sets of modes distinct in acoustical character yet comparable in musical function. They worked to separate the two pitches of each bell by excluding common qualities. For instance, when the *sui* position is struck, the faces and sides of the bell experience the greatest movement and the *gu* areas in between represent the silent, motionless nodes. The *sui* areas become nodes when the bell receives a blow at the *gu* position. Hence, each striking position falls at the point that is least disturbed when the other position is struck, which is also the area least involved in producing the alternate tone.

In order to locate so precisely the nodal meridians of the two fundamental modes, the ancient Chinese must have possessed a theoretical grasp of the physics of music far beyond historians' initial estimates. Given such an understanding, it would be fairly straightforward, although not easy, to find the strike positions that isolate the fundamentals. To achieve the best resolution between pitches, however, overtones as well as fundamentals should be separated. Nodal meridians for the important *gu* overtone modes converge naturally at the *sui* strike position; therefore, they do not contribute to the *sui* tone. The meridians of *sui* overtone modes, however, do not congregate at the *gu* position, so that traces of *sui* partial could interfere when he *gu* tone is struck. Herein lies the rationale for the arched lip of the *zhong* bell.

When we examined the two sets of normal modes, we found that the arch in the bell lip, by changing the shape of the vibrating "plate," also alters the nodal patterns of the most important *sue* overtones. Because of the arched lip, the *sui* overtone meridians converge at the point designated, not coincidentally, as the *gu* strike position. It is typically three-fifths of the way from the *sui* position to the *xian* ridge. The striking position is so critical to obtaining the proper pitch and tone quality that the ancients made inscriptions on the bells to indicate *sui* and *gu* placement unequivocally. Neither the concave rim design nor the precision in identifying the convergence of notal lines could have been accidental.

The *mei* nipples clustered at the top of all but the highest-register bells are also more than ornamental. They help to balance the strength of the two fundamentals so that their volumes are comparable. More important, the *mei* act as another device to separate the two bell tones. Recent laboratory studies have found that the nipples change the complete overtone structures, or frequency spectra, of *sui* and *gu* tones. The *mei* provide extra weight around the bell shoulders, altering nodal

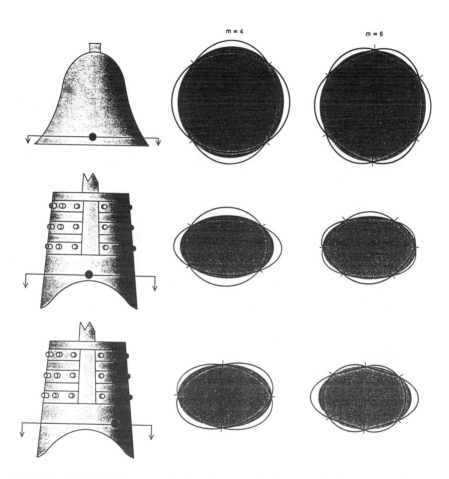

MOTION AT THE RIM when a bell has been struck illustrates the distribution of nodal lines for a round bell *(top)* and for the two pitches of a Chinese *zhong* bell, called *sui (middle)* and *gu (bottom)*. Gray indicates resting positions; lines show changes in the bells's shape after it has been struck. Modes in which *m* is equal to 4 and 6 are represented. At these modes the nodal radii of a round bell are evenly spaced; hence only one patter of distribution is possible. Because a chime bell is oblate, however, a given number of nodal lines can be arranged many different ways and different nodal patterns give rise to different pitches. As is shown here, the patter of nodal radii is determined by the point at which the bell is struck. Chinese designers managed to maximize the separation between the two *zhong* pitches by having the nodal lines of one pitch serve as the striking position for the other.

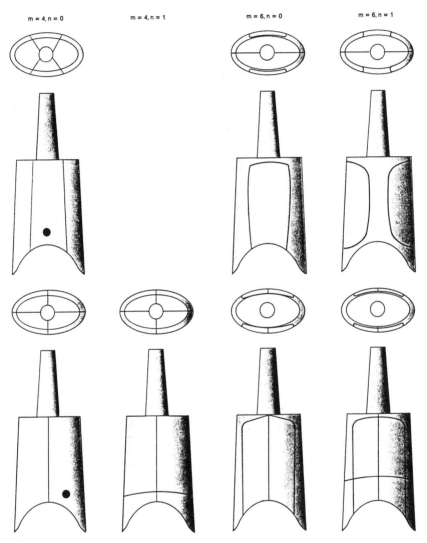

NODAL PATTERNS for the *sui (top)* and *gu (bottom)* pitches describe the modes of the fundamentals and the most conspicuous overtones. Top-view renderings above each bell recall the vibrating-plate system for enumerating radii and circles. Horizontal lines count as circles even when they do no encircle the bell, but near the bell shoulders they do not contribute to the bell's sound and so are not counted. As the top illustration on page 43 shows, the *sui* tone has two dominant overtones and the *gu* tone three.

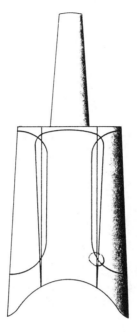

NODAL-LINE CONVERGENCE for the three dominant partial of the *sui* tone is an important consequence of the chime-bell design as found by the authors. If the perimeter of the bell were flat, *sui* nodes would never intersect; hence a blow to any part of the bell would excite at least one *sui* tone. The arched lip of the *zhong* bell, however, rearranges nodal lines so that they congregate at the *gu* position *(circle)*. This convergence helps to clear the *gu* tone of "muddy" *sui* echoes.

patterns in the upper part of the bell. Accordingly they are most pronounced on large bells. Without the *mei*, the *sui* and *gu* fundamentals are easily distinguished, but they have certain high-frequency overtones in common. With the nipples, overtone frequencies shift so that little overlap between the two sets of partial occurs.

The interval between the two pitches on a *zhong* bell is selected by casting and tuning. The choice of the interval is arbitrary, but it should suit the melodic progression of the

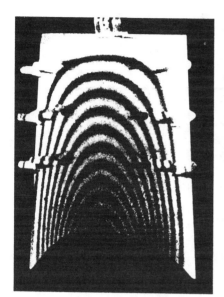

LASER HOLOGRAMS capture the fundamental modes of vibration for the *sui (left)* and *gu (right)* pitches. Wide white areas represent nodes; the dark lines are areas of intense movement. The complementary convergence of nodal lines is apparent. These images result from the differential reflection on light by moving and stationary surfaces of the bell.

compositions it will perform. In addition, the interval should not be a discord since, in spite of the efforts of the designers, traces of the secondary tone may persist after the primary tone has died down. Zhou engineers tuned their bells so that the intervals of the overtones, as well as those of the fundamentals, were harmonic. The second partial of the *gu* tone, for example, is always an octave plus a major or minor third above the *sui* tone; the partial of a *zhong* bell with a minor third separating its two pitches are in the ratio 1:1.2:2.4:2.81:3 and those of a bell with an interval of a major third are 1:1.25:2.5:2.81:3.

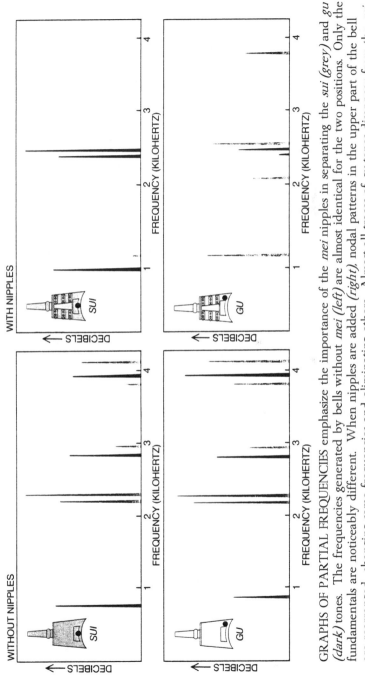

GRAPHS OF PARTIAL FREQUENCIES emphasize the importance of the *mei* nipples in separating the *sui (grey)* and *gu (dark)* tones. The frequencies generated by bells without *mei (left)* are almost identical for the two positions. Only the fundamentals are noticeably different. When nipples are added *(right)*, nodal patterns in the upper part of the bell are rearranged, changing some frequencies and eliminating others. Almost all traces of *gu* tones disappear from the *sui* profile, and only hints of *sui* partial remain in the *gu* tone. *Mei* nipples also serve to increase the volume of the *gu* fundamental so that it matches the volume of the *sui*. This *zhong* bell design is extremely important for optimizing dual-pitched bell performance.

43

Components of the Zhong Bell Tone

Partials	Relative Frequency	Interval with Respect to s(4,0)	Interval with Respect to g(4,0)	Interval with Respect to g^m(4,0)
s(4,0)	1.00		-	-
[g^m(4,0)	1.20	Minor 3rd	-	-]
g(4,0)	1.25	Major 3rd	-	-
[g^m(4,1)	2.40	Octave+ Minor 3rd	-	Octave]
g(4,1)	2.50	Octave+ Major 3rd	Octave	-
g(6,0)	2.81	Octave+ Augmented 4th	Octave+ Major 2nd	Octave+ Minor 3rd
s(6,0)	3.00	12th	Octave+ Minor 3rd	Octave+ Major 3rd

Characterization of the two bell tones shows the relative frequencies of the dominant partials of each tuned bell. The relative component of the partials determines the tone quality of the bell tones. The actual tone quality depends on the accuracy of the positions struck, the force with which the bell is struck and the materials of the striker. We denote partials that are primarily associated with the *sui* position s(m,n), and partials associated with the *gu* g(m,n). For the (4,0) fundamental, two *gu* frequencies are shown; g(4,0) here refers to the major third tuning at the *gu*, and g^m(4,0) in parenthesis refers to the alternative minor third tuning. This covers the apparently preferred bell intervals of the thirds. The frequency ratio of the *gu* tone to the *sui* tone is 1.25 for a bell interval of a major third

OPTIMAL ATTENUATION AND PRISTINE OVERTONE STRUCTURE allow the *bianzhong* bell chime to play complex compositions with individually dual-pitched bells.

and the frequency ratio is 1.20 for a minor third interval. The most important partials are $g(6,0)$ with a frequency 2.25 times that of the $g(4,0)$ fundamental, and $s(6,0)$ with a frequency 3.00 times that of the $s(4,0)$ fundamental. The next partial which shows its dominance in the *gu* tone is $g(4,1)$, at a frequency an octave above the fundamental *gu*. To summarize, the eigenfrequencies of a *zhong* bell with a bell interval of a minor third are in the ratio 1:1.2:2.4:2.81:3, and those of a bell with a bell interval of a major third are in the ratio 1:1.25:2.5:2.81:3. The bell overtones are chosen to be completely consistent with the Chinese concepts of harmony as major 2nd, major 3rd, minor 3rd, augmented 4th, and 12th are all preferred acoustical intervals in Chinese culture.

45

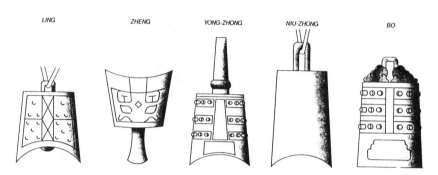

| LING | ZHENG | YONG-ZHONG | NIU-ZHONG | BO |

BELL ANCESTRY suggests the route the ancient Chinese followed arrive at the *zhong* design. The *ling*, oldest of the five bells drawn here, goes back more that 3,600 years. It had a clapper and produced just one unremarkable note. The *zheng* handbell is an early example of the dual-pitch design; it was used by Chinese soldiers, who carried it mouth up. The *niu-zhong* also produces two pitches, but it lacks the clarity of the popular *yong-zhong* at low registers. *Niu-zhong* are visible in the top tier of the chime on page 29. Another *zhong* contemporary, the *bo* served as a monotone ceremonial bell. The bells are not drawn to scale.

When bell-chime intervals from several periods are compared, a historical trend toward the major- and minor-third intervals represented in Marquis Yi's bell collection becomes apparent. Lacking examples of ancient music, one can only assume that this preference matches a taste for major an minor thirds in the musical composition of the time. In Europe, these intervals were not recognized as harmonic until the 12th century.

When Marquis Yi's *bian-zhong* was found, its bells were almost perfectly tuned in spite of their prolonged burial. A second set of 36 bells discovered in the same principality of Zeng in 1981 were even better tuned. Ordinarily a vibrating plate is tuned by the addition or removal of material, but with this method it would seem impossible to tune one bell pitch without altering the other, since both are contained on one continuous body. How did the Chinese tune two pitches on a single *zhong* bell?

Again, the ancients made use of their remarkable expertise in pinpointing nodal lines. They could tune just one pitch by paring bronze off a bell's inner surface if, in paring, they carefully followed the nodal lines of the other. Hence, tuning the *sui* pitch entailed removing metal from the *gu* nodal lines, and vice versa. At the same time, may bells were cast so accurately that they required no modification.

The methodology of bronze casting with pottery sectional molds was fully developed in ancient China. Even so, manufacturing a low‑register *zhong* bell presented quite a formidable task. Large, complicated objects were often made by casting separate parts, the uniting the components in a final mold. But the bronze chime bell, no matter how large, was always cast as a single piece.

In the modern world, the closest approximation of a Chinese bell chime is the carillon. A carillon consists of a group of bells carefully selected to yield equal‑tempered chromatic intervals. The bells are played from a keyboard. Because some of the partial are in discord, only a limited number of chords are within the carillon's scope, and ordinarily only a single melody is played. Considerable knowledge and skill are needed to render satisfactory effects; even expensive installations can give disappointing performances. If the carillon is the best that modernity has to offer, one might wonder how the Chinese arrived at the *bian-zhong* design so long ago.

Since ancient times Chinese musicians have been sensitive to subtle differences in tonal quality. This sensitivity is manifested in many of their instruments. For example, I once asked a Chinese wind player about the design rationale of the *shuang-guan*, an oboe consisting of two apparently identical cylindrical oboes. He replied, "No two reeded tubes have the same tonal spectrum. With two tubes on the *shuang-guan*, the player has control over a broader range of tonality and can be more selective of the timbre."

Perhaps this heightened sensitivity to tonal structure led the ancient Chinese to experiment with a slightly elliptical bell design, which gives rise to a fuller set of vibrational modes and a broader range of overtone possibilities. *Ling* bells, relics of the early Shang period, were oblate but still had clappers and produced only one tone; their musical character can be inferred from the fact that they were used as bells for dogs and cows.

In subsequent efforts the Chinese may have struggled with oblate bells that sounded two distinctly different pitches but produced only awkward or muddy tones. The large, oblate *zheng* handbell, which predates the chime bell by hundreds of years, exemplifies this stage of development. Indeed, *zheng* bells lend their name to the upper half of the *zhong* bell, and the *yong* nose that holds the *zhong* at a 30-degree tilt is derived from the *zheng* bell, however, has a muddy *gu* tone because its flattened mouth does not force the convergence of *sui* nodal lines.

With modification of the bell's surface, cross section and thickness, the two pitches were brought into a well-defined harmonic relation and their individual tones were sharpened; eventually, the sophisticated *zhong* design emerged. Contemporaries of the *zhong* bells include the *niu-zhong*, which is also dual-pitched, and the ceremonial *bo*, which lacks the musical agility of the *zhong*. Both these bells are played in the vertical position.

The art of music[2] has a long and distinguished history that parallels the rise of human civilization. The principles embodied in the Zenghou Yi bell chime suggest that the science of music may have a history almost as long, and just as distinguished. China in the Shang and Zhou periods possessed a level of acoustical science that was essential in supporting the elaborate musical art of those periods. Physics and engineering worked hand in hand to perfect wind, string and percussion instruments and to arrive at orchestration. These are accomplishments that have modern counterparts. In contrast, the overall design of a large set of dual-pitch bells for the performance of music is an achievement that has no equal in the modern physics of music.

---

[2]The other silk & bamboo ensemble instruments, and orchestral instruments are discussed in Lee Yuan-Yuan, The Music of the Zenghou Zhong, *Chinese Music*, **3**, 3 (1980), Lee Yuan-Yuan, An Amazing Discovery in Chinese Music, *Chinese Music*, **2**, 16, (1979) and other papers by Lee.

■

Reeded Winds - the Sounds of the Guanyue

GUANZI: THE WORLD'S OLDEST DOUBLE REED

When working with wind instruments of China, the first instrument that comes to mind is the *guanzi*. The *guanzi*, or *guan*, is a Chinese classical wind instrument with a illustrious history of performance arts and a very strong personality. It is the only double reed classical instrument of its kind in the world that uses a large "unflattened" double reed and an extremely resonant hard tube. As soon as I think of the sound of the *guanzi*, I immediately remember the image of Li Guoying playing "Wailful Wrath by the River" (Jiang He Shui) under the direction of Peng Xiuwen in the 1970s. The *guanzi* tone was so deep and so powerful that its overtone spectrum penetrates the most complex orchestral spectra. This is a reed that goes in and out of his mouth with a shrill voice that genuinely extends that of the human. Another version called the *shuangguan*[1] uses two nominally identical *guanzi* played side by side. I wrote a number of years ago regarding this cultural acoustical requirement - even

---

[1] In fact, the shuangguan was the preferred instrument in recordings made in the 1950s of "Wailful Wrath by the River" (Jiang He Shui). But Li Guoyin's recording on the guanzi under the direction of Peng Xiuwen is todate the best.

GUANYUE PERFORMANCE in Hebei in 1949 - Wang Xiaoshou plays the *haidi*, Wang Tiechui plays the *guanzi*, and Wu Feng plays the *suona* as part of an ensemble (Photo first appeared in Vol. 8, No. 1 of the *Chinese Music* international journal).

though the two *guanzi* in the *shuangguan* are nominally identical, no two tubes/reeds are ever completely identical in overtones; the artist thus has available to him two sets of slightly dissimilar overtones to play with in achieving the final tone at any one time! Such is the cultural acoustical requirements of the Chinese musician.

The orchestra role of the *guanzi* has been ascertained since the Sui-Tang period when its popularity as a classical instrument also propagated to Korean regions. Today it is classified under the broad *shengguan* spectrum. In *shengguan*

SHUANGGUAN PERFORMANCE by Hu Hai-quan.

orchestration, the voice of the *guan* is extremely important, as its cylindrical overtones contrast with the conical overtones of the *suona* family and the free-reed tones of the *sheng* family. The versatility and intrigue of this group is incredible. Peng Xiuwen used it to play "Pictures at the Exhibition" with great success (with a new acoustics, of course). Today younger composers have not quite caught on to the cultural acoustics we are referring to here - and thus the shengguan spectrum is frequently incomplete in their works!

There is in current use a wide variety of sizes of *guanzi* according to lengths and diameters. The common versions are the *xiaoguan*, the *zhongguan*, the *daguan*, and the *jiajianguan*. The

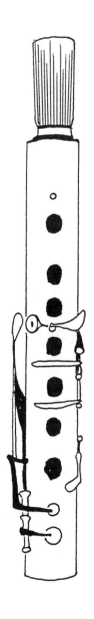

xiaoguan is also known as the soprano *guan*. Its body is short and slender, with a very shrill voice. Its voice depends greatly on performance skill, and produces noise with inferior players. It is frequently a solo instrument in an orchestral passage, and is used to alternate with solo on the *suona*. Another version is the mezzo-soprano *guan*, a fourth lower than the *xiaoguan*, and popular in orchestras. The *zhongguan* is a mid-register wind instrument. It is an octave lower than the *xiaoguan* and has a bright rounded voice. It is the version most useful in shengguan orchestration. The *daguan* is the low *guan*. Its body is long and thick. Its voice is deep and loud, and is one octave lower than the *zhongguan*. It is extremely important in dynamic beats during orchestral phrasing. The *jiajianguan* (left) is a version of the mezzo-soprano *guan* with mechanical keys. It became popular since the 1960s. The ranges of the versions described are: *xiaoguan* a^1-c^4, mezzo-soprano *guan* e^1-a^3, *zhongguan* a-d^3, *daguan* A-d^2, and *jiajianguan* e^1-a^3. The *xiaoguan* is characterized by a tight high range and a broad low range. Its mid range is the

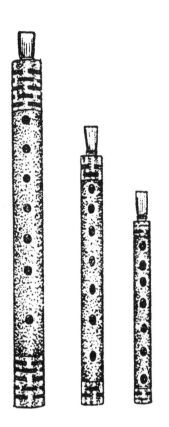

brightest and the easiest to use in orchestra and is extremely expressive. In the orchestral acoustics of the orchestras of Hebei, Shanxi, Xian, Beijing and Fujian, the *daguan* and the *xiaoguan* are very common. The *xiaoguan* plays rapid passages that are celebratory and lively. The *daguan* is lyrical. Frequently, the *daguan* and the *xiaoguan* each take the lead. Sometimes two *xiaoguan* are played contrapuntally. Even more interesting is the combined acoustics of the *daguan*, the *xiaoguan* and the orchestra all taking part at the same time. In addition to regular ranges, each guan may alter its range by the use of alternative reeds. It is one of the most dynamic classical wind instruments.

Coming back to the perspective of geography-specific acoustics, the *guanzi* is still nominally a northern sound. In the south we use the *houguan* version, which is a lot softer in timbre and uses a horn. The bass *houguan* is quite versatile in its orchestrational use and is today absorbed into many different orchestras all over China. The regular *houguan* is still popular in

Reeded Winds

Cantonese orchestras and ensembles of Cantonese music (Guangdong Yinyue), and speaks a Cantonese voice. In popular pieces such as "The Peacock Spreads Its Tail", the presence of the sound of the southern *houguan* is always a must.

The *guan* was the earliest double-reed musical instrument in the world. It has a cylindrical air column made of either wood, bamboo, or tin. Both ends of the air column have molded onto them tin rings. An incompletely flattened reed is attached to the upper end of the column for performance. Eight or nine finger holes are usually used. The *guan* is incredibly expressive and has been an important orchestral instrument since ancient times. The *Book of Songs* mentions the *guan* and the *xiao* (panpipe) together in Zhou courts. *Lushi Chunqiu* describes a Xia court performance in which the *guan*, the *xiao*, the bell, the drum and the stone chime entertained an amazed audience. Tang poets have documented the moving performances of the *guan* by the renowned soloist, An Wan-shan, and his skills in modulation.

The *guan* has been in use in orchestras all over China but is considered a difficult instrument to learn. It is said "if it takes a hundred days to learn the *sheng*, it will take a thousand for the *guan*,..." Most players learn the artistry over a long period of time by participating since early childhood in music associations known as "Chuige Hui". "Chuige" means wind music and "Hui" is a club. When my good friend Wang Tiechui was little he was fascinated by the *guan* performances in farm concerts. At early age he studied the instrument and participated in the popular concerts. The repertoire that he was exposed to was very broad in the "Chuige" clubs and with masters, including large instrumental suites, classical compositions and folk tunes. He was totally moved by the energy of the performances and their musical charm. Solo repertoire concentrated on the voice quality since many compositions originated in Hebei Clapper Opera, Old-tune String Music, Kun Opera, Peking Opera and so on. In the orchestral "*chui-ge*", the *guan* is often called "*tou-guan*" (lead *guan)* as it is the lead instrument. The *sheng,* the *guan,* the *di* and the *suona* all play different roles, each having its own orchestration effect. The *suona* often dominates the middle and the low registers. The *guan* and the *di* play high, and the *middle* register parts. The double-reeds and the reeded *di* use short notes and extended notes to complement the melody and harmony of the free-reeded *sheng.* The performance is usually improvisational. The mutual understanding between players is at the highest level. The music is colorful, lively and youthful, and is the favorite of Norther Chinese peasants. In 1949 Wang Tiechui was invited to play "Herding the Donkey", a Hebei Chuige composition, at the First Cultural Convention and Wang was well received. During that time many *guan* performers joined cultural institutions and the artistry became known all over again in China. Liu Guan-yue performed in Europe. Yin Er-wen, Meng Qing-yun, Hu Hai-quan and others popularized classical composition such as "The Willow is Green", "The Solo Flying Tune", "Sawing the Water Vessel", "Wailful Wrath by the River" and others, broadening the concert scene. Zhang Ji-gui has been modifying the instrument and composing new pieces. Hu Hai-quan composed and performed "Ode to Autumn". His

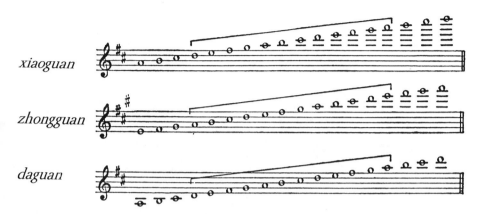

xiaoguan	
zhongguan	
daguan	

COMPASS & NOTES SEQUENCE of the three common *guanzi*. Ranges marked cover the region that is most expressive, colorful and most commonly used.

mellow tone led listeners into the dream world of Bai Ju-yi's poetry. Wu Xiao-zhong had his own version of "Three Verses of Yangguan". Yin Wei-jun of the Central Traditional Orchestra played "The Joyous Yan-bian", offering the unique mood of music from the Changbai Mountain. Hu Zhi-hou of the Central Conservatory wrote works for the *guan* and orchestra.

THE HARMONIZING SHENG & THE MELODIC YU

In the name "shengguan" for wind acoustics is the *sheng*.

The *sheng* and the *yu* are the other half of the shengguan spectrum. The *sheng* is today's most popular free-reed mouth organ. The names "*yu*" and "*he*" were popular during the Yin Shang period (16th-11th BC). "*Yu*" appeared more frequently than "*he*". Both "*yu*" and "*he*" belonged to the *sheng* family. The *yu* is

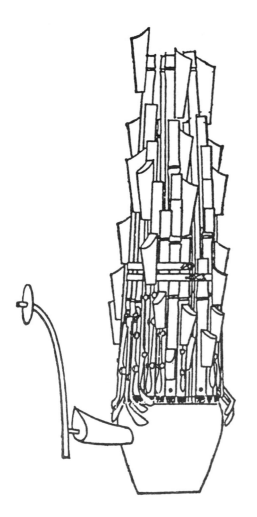

THE *SHENG* AND THE *YU* were the first musical instruments in the world utilizing a coupled free reed/air column acoustical system. The *yu* was the first musical instrument to employ a u-tube system to bend air column while minimizing acoustical mismatch. The *sheng* is today still the only wind instrument that plays harmony.

a melodic instrument. It sounded "yu-yu" in voice to the ancient Chinese, and thus its name. The *lusheng* of the Miao Nationality has the mouth piece going through rows of reeded pipes. This is the ideographic origin of the word *yu*". The square *fangsheng* today has two major groups of pipes, and this coincides with the ideogram *yu* with two representative rows.

The *he* is a musical instrument that harmonizes, thus the name *he*". Today, the name *he* is still used. The well-known *sheng* artist Hu Tian-quan says "in my home town, the Qi village in Qi County of Shanxi, the fourteen-reed *sheng* is called the *he*". In the development of

Reeded Winds

Chinese wind instruments, as in the development of other classes of instruments, melodic and harmonic instruments are used in parallel. In the case of the mouth organ, the *yu* plays complex melodies, while the *sheng* harmonizes with harmonic intervals and chords which are harmonic or inharmonic according to the harmonic basis used in the passage. The *chi* played harmonic intervals and the *di* played complex melody as flutes. The reason for this complementarity, which is always so complete, lies in the basic nature of Chinese music, built on harmony. Melodic progression, temperament theory, and orchestration follow the same harmonic system - as parts of the same cultural acoustics. Thus there was no need in Chinese music to develop scale and harmony separately, as is the case of western music. The notion of the scale does not even have to exist in Chinese music. But the five complete harmonic skeletons of *zhi, shang, yu, jue,* and *gong* dominate music making (Shen, 1981), and temperament choice and orchestration complement each other in real-life applications. The Chinese cultural acoustics is thus driven by the central concept of harmony.

The reed provides the material foundation for the *sheng* and the free reed appeared during very early stage of the Chinese civilization. The original free reed was made of bamboo. Many mount-string type instruments in Southwestern China still utilize these free-reed systems. The *sheng* was developed on the basis of the "*huang*" free reed, and is the first coupled air column-free reed system in a musical instrument.

During Western Zhou (11th Century-771 BC), musical art developed to the point that musical instruments were classified according to acoustical materials. Eight basic acoustical materials were recognized. The *sheng* was classified as a gourd. This is further confirmed by the unearthed instruments in the tombs of Zenghouyi and at Ma Wang Dui.

When the rulers of Western Zhou held wine-tasting festivities, the *sheng* was used for its music. Several instrumental pieces used for this purpose are known today. They are entitled "Nan Gai", "Bai Hua", and "Hua Shu". When the rulers practiced archery, the *sheng* was played with the stone chime and the bell chime. Its harmonizing role was prominent. *The Book of Songs* also refers to "blowing the *sheng* and playing the reed" in music making with mouth organs.

The *sheng* and the *yu* were extremely popular in the Spring and Autumn (770-476 BC) and the Warring States (475-221 BC) periods. This was a period of rapid development of arts and sciences in China, and the music of the *sheng* penetrated into all levels of music making.

Su Qin told the Xuan Emperor of Qi that "in the affluent cities, all citizens play the *yu*, the *se* (large horizontal open-string zither), the *zhu* (string instrument with fingerboard struck with a bow), and the *qin* (fingerboarded zither)". The book *Han Feizi* recorded that the Xuan Emperor of Qi (319-301 BC) used the *yu* orchestras "three-hundred strong" which documented the large size of the *yu* orchestras used then.

The musical treasures of Zenghouyi revealed the orchestral structure of two orchestras of the Yangzi river region. The *shengs* with gourd mouth pieces and bamboo pipes and reeds were among the large number of musical instruments in the two orchestras. Panpipes and bamboo flutes were also among the instruments. This confirms the writings in the *Rites of Zhou* "the *sheng* master is in charge of the *yue,* the *yu,* the *sheng,* the *xiao,* the *chi,* the *di,* the *guan,*..."

The *yu* of this period were equipped with thirty six reeds. The *yu* of Ma Wang Dui even used the u-tube principle which allowed long tubes to be of several sections joined by structures minimizing acoustical mismatch. This period thus saw the height in the science of *sheng* manufacturing.

From Han documentation, the *sheng* and *yu* were continuously used in orchestras, but in some cases the number of reeds were reduced to nineteen. There were also mentions of large ones having nineteen reeds and small ones having thirteen reeds.

From the cultural relics unearthed, numerous *sheng* and *yu* type instruments were available. The number of reeds or tubes had indeed decreased from the Spring and Autumn and the Warring States Periods. The two well-known *yu* of Ma Wang Dui have twenty-two and twenty-six pipes respectively. As mentioned before, the u-tube principle is fully employed here. Some u-tubes are 80 cm in effective length and are suitable for generating rather low pitches. The pipes were also arranged in layers. The outer layer pipes have two fingerholes in some cases, allowing both layers to be played at the same time or independently. If it were not for these relics, such acoustical design may be lost forever.

During Sui and Tang, orchestral music was developed to a very high point. Various string instruments including the *pipa*, the *wuxian*, the *ruan*, the *zheng*, the *konghou* and others were popular both as solo and orchestral instruments. As far as wind instrument in the orchestra goes, the *xiao*, the *di*, the *luguan*, the *bili (guan)* and others took over the dominant position of the sheng family. During the ruling period of the Wen Emperor of Tang (827-840), the *yu* gradually faded into the *Yunshao Yayue* ancient music category. At the Northern Song period (960-1127), the *yu* was gone, and the *sheng* remained with nineteen reeds, seventeen reeds, and thirteen reeds. During Ming, Qing and the Republic, the *yu* was long gone, and even the nineteen reed *sheng* was rare. Today both the roles of the *yu* and the *sheng* are back, in the various sizes and orchestral roles written and played for the 26-reed and 36-reed *sheng*.

THE SYSTEM OF GUANYUE WIND INSTRUMENTS

The comprehensive system of the *guanyue*, the Chinese winds, was studied during the last three decades by the Music Research Institute of the Chinese Music Society of North America. The study covered the excitation types for these wind instruments, resonator types, resonator shapes, and coupled system types. We focused in particular on the ensemble and orchestral acoustics when these instruments are employed.

Reeded Winds

26-Reed Bass   36-Reed Midrange   36-Reed High

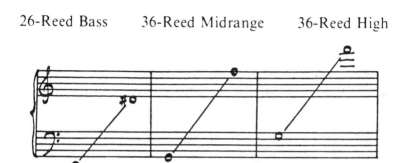

THE SHENG FAMILY today cover both the functions of the melodic yu and the harmonizing sheng and is the most powerful group of wind instruments in probably any orchestra.

The Chinese instrument makers and artists experimented with gradually varying methods of air column excitation and air-column coupling, thus creating the most complete resonators for wind instruments and the most complete techniques for wind performance. Their heightened sensitivity to tonal structure produced the most sophisticated coupled systems used in wind resonators and a most unique school of performing arts of wind instruments anywhere.

The Chinese loves the full-bodied tone of the large air column and the high frequencies of the short and narrow air column. They also love the contrast between tones of the air column and the most sensitively coupled systems of free reed and air column, and coupled systems of air column and reeded excitation. The oldest group of end-blown flutes known in the world is 8,000 years old. This type of flute was unearthed in the twentieth century (Huang, 1989) and found to contain the complete interval preferences of Chinese music. The end-blown

THE SIDE-BLOWN FLUTE was invented in China and is the most popular flute in the world today.

flute utilizes the edge effect -- when a controlled thin stream of air breaks on a sharp edge. Bottle blowers uses this same principle to excite the resonances of the air contained in a bottle. In the end-blown flute, the length of the air column, cylindrical in the *dongxiao* and slightly conical in the *chiba* (meaning "a foot and eight inches" in length), is altered by fingering to produce the required fundamental interval relations, and by overblowing. When different lengths of end-blown pipes are used together, the *paixiao* panpipe is formed. In the last dynasty, the Qing dynasty of China, revivalist activities were prevalent without much musical substance. Ancient instruments were reconstructed by the Qing court according to temperament systems believed to be true and practical without considerations of what musical performance really is and really require. Thus replicas of so-called ancient instruments were produced for the Qing court and for use in ceremonial settings. In particular, the *paixiao* and the *bianzhong*, two ancient instruments in the panpipe and in the bell chime family, were reproduced with totally wrong design. The *bianzhong* replica of the Qing court used bells with round cross-section, which in the face of current research is complete ignorance (see Chapter on musical bell

Reeded Winds

THE *PAIXIAO* PANPIPE FROM 5TH CENTURY BC among the Zenghou Yi musical treasures is arranged according to the heptatonic (seven-tone) steps and is thus practical for performance of music of the period as well for music today.

chimes). The *paixiao* reconstructed used a chromatic arrangement with pitches derived from the method of trisection. The *paixiao* discovered in the Zenghou Yi collection (see Lee, 1978) emphasized neighboring minor thirds and major seconds, and further all Zenghou Yi instruments were not tuned to the method of trisection which had been superseded by more superior methods emphasizing physically just intervals.

Understanding and utilizing the resonance of an air column, whether cylindrical, conical, or a combination of both, appeared more than 8,000 years ago. The earliest eight-holed vertical flute, which was recovered in the twentieth century, is 8,000 years old. These vertical flutes principally utilize the edge-effect, which is the bottle-blowing technique many cultures have come to know and love. The development of the practice of musical performance on a single air column by opening successive holes on the body of a flute containing the air column and the practice of musical performance on a series of air columns of successively shorter length apparently developed in parallel. The end-blown bone flute of 8,000 years ago was already so well developed that it contained eight open holes for the performance of all harmonic intervals and two registers. Harmonic intervals are a function of culture. The Chinese culture has a much larger set of preferentially accepted harmonic intervals than the west. It has also invented the resonator systems needed to produce tone qualities and a pitch space now recognized as incredibly complete. The pitch of music is determined by how quickly the vibrating element (reed, air column, string, membrane, etc.) in the instrument and the air which transmits it are vibrating at. For a low note, the air vibrates slowly. For example in playing a C_o, a musician vibrates air at 16 cycles per second. A high note vibrates rapidly. The now internationally accepted A_4 vibrates at 440 cycles per second. Registers and intervals are subdivisions of the audible range. Registers divide the audible range into broad areas the size of octaves. Intervals are a more exact measure of pitch-to-pitch distance throughout the range. Pitches are the same distance (interval) apart when the frequency ratio of the notes involved are the same. The globular flute, *xun*, of 7,000 years ago emphasized a minor third interval. The *xun* fascinated the west with its intervals (see e.g. Creel, 1937). The *paixiao* (panpipe) of China and the *sheng* month organ belong to the other family which utilized bamboo pipes of various lengths, with the *paixiao* using edge-effect excitation and the *sheng* family using perfect matches of free reed and air column.

The *sheng* comes in both open-tube and closed-tube types. In the smaller *sheng*, each air column in resonance with its free reed is usually open at the top. Each pipe contains a finger hole which when closed sets the pipe in resonance with its free reed, and when open no resonance takes place. The free reed in the bottom of each pipe only partially seals the air blown in when the finger hole is not closed. In larger *sheng* and the *yu*, closed pipes are used to conserve air. Each pipe is closed by a key when not fingered. When fingered, the key opens and the air column is set in to resonance with the free reed. The closed pipe system is thus more energy conserving. The principles of acoustical mismatch are widely used in the design of the *sheng*, the *yu*, and their accessories (CMSNA, 1980).

The development of Chinese instrumental music benefited from the continuity of the interacting branches of Chinese culture - those of the Yangzi River region, those of the Pearl River region, those of the Yellow River region, those of the Yili River region, and others. Instruments and tonal qualities have come and gone, but the available acoustical systems and accumulated aesthetic appreciation for sound and music persisted. Some have said that Chinese music never developed after a certain point in history, e.g. during or after the Song Dynasty. This is in a sense true for all of the main resonator types and the preference of intervals appeared to have gone through several complete cycles before.

There are many exceptions of course to this observation, which is by no means complete. The development and blossoming of silk and bamboo music is one critical development which defines an important part of Chinese musical art forms today (University of California, 1990).

The transverse flute represents a major breakthrough in the understanding of musical acoustics in the history of mankind. A similar breakthrough is the use of U-tubes in the design of the pipes of wind instruments such as the mouth organs the *sheng* and the *yu*. The principle common to all wind instruments is that of an air volume defined by a resonator body. The resonance in the resonator is the source of the sound. This sound becomes music when melodies or harmonies can be produced. In the case of the ancient Chinese instrument the *he* and the *sheng*, harmony is primarily produced. In the case of the *xiao*, the *paixiao*, the *suona*, the *yu*, the oboe, the clarinet, the piccolo, the saxophone, and most other wind instrument including brass instruments, melody is produced. All of the wind instrument listed here are end blown, whether through a reed, a mouthpiece, or through the edge effect directly.

The transverse flute is called *hengdi, dizi*, or simply *di* in China. Nowadays the most common flute in the world is the transverse flute. The first transverse flute first appeared in China (Meylan, 1988), and apparently the early Chinese transverse flutes were held to the left. Today most flute players learn to play holding the flute to the right. The best known Chinese masters, however, still hold their *di* to the left (refer to the transverse flute performance of Lu Chun-ling and Wang Tiechui, for example).

The appearance of the transverse flute in China represented a major scientific breakthrough. Utilization of the edge effect in the end-blown vertical flute is natural. Appreciating that the edge effect could be utilized at an edge on a hole on the body of the flute represents the understanding a major acoustical concept - that side-blown excitation can be as effective or more effective than end-blown excitation. Such conceptual developments are plentiful in *guanyue* development. The earliest side-blown flute was recognized by the flute master Zhao Song-ting (see Qu, 1989) when he studied the bone flutes of Hemudu from 7,000 years ago. In the development of the mouth organs the *sheng* and the *yu*, the U-tube was further discovered where small acoustical impedances were used in using air columns which did not have to be straight and were allowed to bend (Shen, 1982).

Two types of transverse flutes were popular in China: the *chi* which is a closed-tube system, sealed at the right end and usually played with the instrument held to the right, and the *di* which is an open-tube system described above, often held to the left. Since the discovery of the Zenghou Yi musical treasures of the 5th century BC, the *chi* has been studied more thoroughly than previously. The *chi* in the Zenghou Yi version is an interval instrument performing harmonic skeletons emphasizing the preferred interval of minor third. It is held with both hands on the outside of the *chi*. Two versions of this transverse flute have been observed. The Zenghou Yi version with the five finger holes to the right and the air hole on the left is more common (see Lee, 1979 and Lee, 1980). Another version has the finger hole in the middle of the *chi*, as described by Needham (Needham, 1962) and as seen in artifacts from the Yangjiawan archeological find of Changsha in Hunan Province. The *di* has usually six finger holes and is played with crossed fingering for complex melodies, and is the ancestor of the modern flute and the *modi*, the *di* with reed membrane on its body for additional unstable coupling to give the typical Chinese bamboo flute tonal spectrum.

The transverse flute moved through central Asia to Europe, and today all flute players play the transverse flute. The vertical end-blown flute utilizing the edge effect is less known to the west. Vertical end blown flute with a flue is popular in the west and is call the recorder in the west. The flue ensures that the excitation is always controlled and thus instruments with a flue are much easier to play. But the masterly control by good players is what makes end-blown flute without flues what they are musically. They are a whole class above the recorder family in terms of tonal spectrum possibilities and their performance is totally dependent on the skill and the musicianship of the player.

The open-tube transverse flute developed in China through two major acoustical designs: the first with no membrane coupling as in the *chi* and the *hengxiao,* the second with active participation of a reed membrane as in the *modi,* or today's *di* (*dizi*).

The *paixiao* panpipe and the *sheng* differ in their methods of excitation, and two entirely different Instruments were invented. Both instruments utilize different lengths of air columns. The different-lengthed pipes of the *paixiao* are excited by the edge effect and therefore depend greatly on embouchure. Each of the *sheng* pipes is a coupled system of a reed (a free reed unconstrained) and air column. The reed's frequency of vibration matches exactly that corresponding to the height of the air column. Each pipe of the *sheng* is thus a much more sophisticated music maker than the pipes on the *paixiao*, thus the unique stimulating sound of the *sheng* pipes in all ranges. In the high range, the high-frequency reed quality dominates, and the sheng is often described as "slightly metallic" in this range. Towards the lower range, the voice of the air column dominates. There the music of the *sheng* is very much an interestingly modified full-bodied air column.

In the *di* flute family, the change in pitch is accomplished by changes in the length of air columns configured by fingering a single cylindrical chamber (the flute body). With appropriately placed holes on the flute body, player's fingers control how much of the air in the cylindrical tube is set into vibration. The *di* further modified the vibration of the air set into vibration by the incorporation of a reed membrane on the body of the tube containing the air column. This membrane therefore must be placed between the air inlet and the first hole, so that all fingering configurations will include the membrane in the path of air vibration.

The single free reed family of instruments is a combination of both types of resonators used in the transverse flute and the *sheng*. The very popular *bawu* is a flute (with series of finger holes), supported by a triangular free reed, which depresses itself into different positions allowing a large range of quantized free reed frequencies to be generated in resonance with the length of active air column set into vibration by the control of fingering. The single free-reed cannot be overblown effectively, like the case of the single cane reed, such as that on the chalumeau.

The *bawu* is therefore played without the edge effect. While playing, the player's mouth completely covers the mouthpiece which contains the reed, a triangular tongue cut out of a thin piece of brass, the tongue being the sing free reed capable of many different levels of depression in free vibration coupled to the vibration of the air column. When the *bawu* is not played, the triangular tongue stays above the brass frame out of which it was cut, the cut being along the equal sides of the isosceles triangle. The base of the triangle is not cut and the base serves as the flexible that bends during the free ringing vibration.

Few wind instruments have such a variety of tonal coloring by the player as the *guanzi*, or the saxophone.

COMPLEMENTARITY OF INSTRUMENTS: HARMONY AND MELODY

From the above discussion, it is obvious that in the development of wind instruments, as in the development of other classes of instruments, melodic and harmonic instruments are used in parallel. In the case of the mouth organ, the *yu* plays complex melodies, while the *sheng* harmonizes with harmonic intervals and chords which are harmonic or inharmonic according to the harmonic basis used in the passage. The *chi* played harmonic intervals and the *di* played complex melody as flutes. The reason for this complementarity, which is always so complete, lies in the basic nature of Chinese music, which is built on harmony from day one. Melodic progression, temperament theory, and orchestration follow the same harmonic system - as parts of the same cultural acoustics. Thus there was no need in Chinese music to develop scale and harmony separately, as is the case of western music. The notion of the scale does not even exist in Chinese musical literature. But the five complete harmonic skeletons of *zhi, shang, yu, jue,* and *gong* dominate music making (Shen, 1981), and temperament choice and orchestration complement each other in real-life applications. The Chinese cultural acoustics is thus driven by harmony, perhaps much more so than any other culture.

MUSIC OF THE DOUBLE REED

The most popular group of wind instrument in history is the end-blown flutes. The second most popular group is the double reed. There are two distinct double-reed sub-groups, which are acoustically based on the following systems:

SUONA PERFORMANCE BY HAO YUQI - Hao is a master of the *haidi* and the *suona*. He was featured in Vol. 11, No. 2 of the *Chinese Music* international journal.

(A)   The first group uses flattened double reeds. This group includes the *suona*, the *haidi*, the shawm and the oboe. The player excites the vibration of the air column by first exciting the squeaky sound of the double reed which is flattened. The music that is produced is a result of the sound of the reed, the sound of the air column in close coupling.

(B)   The second group uses large and unflattened double reeds. The full-bodied *guan*, or *guanzi*, uses an "unflattened" double reed - a totally different concept compared with the double reeds. Here the reed is only flattened near the tip. As the player performs, he moves continuously in and out of the unflattened region. The unflattened part of the reed is critical in producing the most human sound of the *shuangguan, guanzi,* producing the most human sound of the *shuangguan, guanzi, houguan,* and the bass *houguan.* Here the large reed itself, up to more than three quarters of an inch in width and two to three times that in length is a double reed as well as a strongly resonating air resonator. It couples integrally with the air column of the wooden pipe in performance. The *shuangguan* has two double-reeded double pipes. The *guanzi,* the *houguan* and the bass *houguan* all utilize a single non-flattened double reed coupled to a cylindrical air column shaped by a highly resonant wooden cylinder. This group of double reed instruments is unfamiliar to musicians of the west. Many western studies merely mention the *guanzi* as a double reed in the same class as the *suona* due to lack of familiarity with this type of instrument (see e.g. Joppig, 1988). The reed of the *guanzi* as discussed above serves two functions. It is both the source of excitation and also a major part of the resonator.

My conversation with a Chinese wind player about the design rationale of the *shuangguan,* which consists of two apparently identical cylindrical *guanzi,* is now well known. As no two reeded tubes have the same tonal spectrum-with two tubes on the shuangguan, the player has control over a broader range of tonal quality and can be more selective of the timber (Shen, 1987).

Double-piped instruments for this reason of tonal spectrum are very popular in Chinese and other music. Hayashi Kenzo in his studies of instruments said that "if both pipes produce the same sound, there is no need for two in a group" and he, of course, completely missed the point.

The extremely high sensitivity to tonal structure led the ancient Chinese to experiment with gradually varying methods of air column excitation and air-column coupling, thus creating the most complete set of resonators and techniques for music of the winds.

The amplified coupled system of the *lusheng* (right) is another fabulous invention. Nowadays its principles are incorporated in many orchestral *sheng* and *yu*.

SUONA: THE CONICAL DOUBLE REED

The *suona* is today the most popular double-reed wind instruments of China. Compared with the *guan*, it has the flattened reed. Although not as old as the *guan*, it has been popular for over seventeen hundred years. From studies of musician figurines performing the *suona* in the Yungang Grottoes of Shanxi and the Kezier Grottoes of Xinjiang, we found the *suona* to be popular in the two Jin periods (265-420). In 1978 musicians studied the Yungang Grottoes and focused on *suona* musicians in the 10th cave Zhao & Shen, 1988). The second musician from the left on the north wall was playing the *suona*, a version similar to the present-day wooden *suona*. This cave was built between 484 and 489. The 38th cave of Kezier Grottoes also contained painted musicians playing the *suona*, a version similar to the Yungang version. This cave was built between 265 and 420. During the two Jin periods, the city of Datong, Shanxi Province, was a center of political, economic and religious development and the *suona* was one of the popular instruments.

Chinese Musical Instruments

Numerous descriptions of *suona* performance and *suona* music appeared in the Ming period literature. The document *Sanchai Tuhui* cites *suona* of the *laba* (trumpet) category as a military and folk instrument. *The Musical Collections of Wang Xilou* by Wang Pan of the Ming period contains the ballad *Chao Tianzi* which describes the physical construction and musical role of the *suona*.

During the Zhengde years (1506-1521) of Ming, the *suona* was both popular in court as well as folk orchestras. It became one of the most popular instruments. Its roles included solo, orchestral, theatrical, and dance accompaniment. As far as festive music was concerned, wind and percussion orchestras and percussion (*luogu*) orchestras both emphasized the use of the *suona*.

During the Qing period, the *suona* was further included in the Hui orchestras by the court.

The *suona* is made up of the following components: a small double reed, an air block, a small copper cone, a main wooden cone, and the flared amplification horn. It is both brass and wood in construction. On the wooden cone we find eight finger holes, seven in front and one in the back. The air that passes through the vibrating tiny reed excites the air cone whose length is controlled by fingering. A wide range of harmonics is stimulated. The usual range of a *suona* covers two octaves plus a major second.

The performance is controlled by air, finger, teeth, tongue, lip, and the throat. The basic playing techniques can be grouped into thirty or more categories. These techniques are used individually as well as in groups. They create the most expressive tone imaginable and became the manners of speech for musical interest. The Chinese people love the *suona*, but for reasons attributable to levels of cultural exposure, many first-time Western listeners can hardly tolerate the *suona*.

During the popularization of the *suona*, different cultural regions produced *suona* of a large number of sizes and tone. They each possess vivid regional flavor and are broadly used in theatrical music, in instrumental repertoire and in song and dance accompaniments.

Musicians performing the *suona* in ancient times were slaves of fuedalism treated merely as musical technicians. Folk musicians used the *suona* for self-entertainment and passed on its artistry within their own schools in a near-oral tradition.

Many scores for the *suona* were passed down from the Ming and the Qing periods. They are in the *gongche* notation. The famous *Twenty Eight Tunes of Northeastern Suona* are now being deciphered.

Those of us who listen to folk compositions regularly will no doubt find *Birds Courting the Phoenix* and *One Magnificent Flower* representative of the improvisational repertoire. Most of these compositions are musically abstract and difficult to comprehend by conservatory musicians.

The artistry of the *suona*, when influenced by theatrical music, becomes highly region-specific. All provinces and all minority nationalities have some form of *suona*. The major schools, however, are clearly characterized.

The Northeastern-styled performance is centered in the Southern part of Liaoning geographically. The popular Hebei-styled performance has its center in Hebei. The Shanxi-styled performance is centered in the Southeastern part of Shanxi Province. The lucid Chaozhou and Guangdong styles are centered in Shantou and Guangzhou.

These main-stream schools are part of everyday life. They employ different ways of expression to show laughter, anger, sadness and joy. Festive occasions and events such as weddings, funerals and others cannot be separated from the *suona*.

Suona music of the Northeastern style is bright and often high-pitched. It is noted for its energy as well as grace. The theatrical component of this school and the dance-music component of this style are often related to the *Errenzhuan* theater and the *Dayangge* folk repertoire. The drum ensemble *Guyue* produced a large number of large-scaled compositions (*Dapaiziqu*). These repertories are reflected in, for example, the *suona* concerto *Celebration of Victory* performed by the *suona* artist Hu Tiangquan in 1956 with the orchestra. It merely gave the music community a little flavor of what is possible with this style.

The Central Plains style is lyrical. Its well-known composition *Birds Courting the Phoenix* had its origin in Shandong Province. All musicians of this style play this piece and other related pieces. Recent *suona* musicians of this style include Liu Fengming of Anhui Province, Xu Jingzhi of Henan Province, and Ren Tongxiang of Shandong Province. Hao Yuqi is a more recent artist from Henan.

The Hebei style is known for its *Chuige* format. The *Chuige* is a "wind song" in which a *suona* leads the orchestra. The compositions utilize the methods of melodic embellishment, natural counterpoint and enormous technical nuances. These can be witnessed in the recordings of the masters Zhao Chunting, Zhao Chunfeng and others.

Often neglected by suona researchers is the Guangdong Shantou style. This suona music is powerful and sentimental. Its repertoire can be found today in the *Zhaozhou Daluogu* percussion orchestra and the *Xiaoluogu* orchestra and in *Guangdong Yinyue*, Cantonese instrumental music. The currently performed version of *Paowang Buyu* (Catching with the Fishing Net) from the percussion orchestra repertoire no longer carries the flavor the the suona performance called for by this piece. *Fendie Caihua* (Butterfly Among Flowers) is from the *Xiaoluogu* branch of this style. This style has not been recorded enough. We encourage the reader to look up recordings by Zhang Tianping, Hu Zhao and Wang Anmin.

The use of the various *suona* in the Chinese orchestras is quite systematic. The status of *suona* performers is also ascertained by society. In the 1960s Liu Fengtong, Wang Chuanyun, Zhang Zongkong, Hu Haiquan and others worked extensively on the mid-register *suona*. For Southern *suona* the noted Cantonese master Zhang Tianping worked on the high-register, the low-register as well as the mid-register *suona*. His *suona* uses a number of air holes ranging from seventeen to more. They are most suited for the classical Guangdong repertoire.

What is indeed lacking today is for professional composers to master the *suona* repertoire. The *suona* is often used in the most simplistic manner imaginable in the so-called modern compositions. The Chinese Music Society of North America works with performers and composers, in such a way that the lasting musical interest of the classics can be appreciated and new works be written in the direction of the advancement of music rather than in the direction of oversimplifying the Chinese orchestra.

GUANYUE & THE USE OF SHENGGUAN ACOUSTICS

The general discussion of resonator types and the specific discussions of resonator design for specific performance practices provide the basis for understanding the rich family of *guanyue* (Chinese wind group). The nomenclature of "*shengguan*" is used in the orchestral practices, and the Chinese wind group forms a very powerful fundamental tonal basis for the Chinese orchestra. This "woodwind" orchestral practice has been a pure instrumental art form for the history of Chinese music, compared with the strictly instrumental use of woodwinds in Western orchestras which appeared only in the 17th Century with the adoption of the oboe (Baines, 1991). In the regional orchestras of China, there is usually one first fiddle and one second fiddle. There are sometime a third and a fourth fiddle as well. The Chinese orchestra does not consist of violins or fiddles as fundamental tonal basis. The fundamental spectrum of the orchestra or the ensemble is usually one of *shengguan* (reeded winds) or *tanbo* (plucked strings). The Chinese Orchestra is thus unique in this sense and the *sheng* and *guan* wind instruments must be properly utilized as a group. In this context, the powerfulness of the *suona* must not be overemphasized (Zhao and Shen, 1988) among the *guanyue* group.

Chinese traditional orchestration places very high emphasis on tonal differences of the acoustical systems, which drive the musical instruments. The *xun* has in the twentieth century reacquired a role it has not enjoyed for hundreds, if not for thousands of years. This globular flute of all sizes and design exemplifies the high level of human creativity in vessel blowing and associated understanding of resonator design. The most natural and most human tone of the *xun* is today appreciated again, now by composers and concert goers as one end of the tonal spectrum, arising from the most complex vibration excited by the simplest edge effect in near-spherical wind chambers. The extent of pitch variation, associated with any one fingering, is particularly useful in playing ancient and modern classics.

The *bili*, one of the most popular member of the *guanzi* family, is at the other end of the tonal spectrum. Its large and long reed is coupled to the straight cylindrical tube made of very-high-density wood. This rare coupled system in musical acoustics history has much simpler acoustics compared with the *xun*, but produced the most powerful and magnetic tone quality that amplified the large and long reed more than the straight air column, producing some of the most unfamiliar sound to modern

Western listeners. And yet when modern Western listeners become accustomed to it, it offers the attractive orchestrational component in Chinese orchestral music. In listening and studying "Wailful Wrath by the River" performed on the *guanzi* by Li Guo-yin, Western trained performers and composers have come to be totally attracted by its tonal magic.

The harmonizing *sheng* mouth organ sits in the middle of the tonal spectrum in the Chinese wind ensemble and many Chinese orchestras. This middle ground is awfully wide in spectral compass. Its voice ranges from free-reed dominated pleasant vibration to air-column dominated full-bodied tube sound. It is never at either extreme occupied by the *xun* or the *guanzi*. For numerous orchestration styles, it serves a harmonizing purpose that is indispensable. In ensemble music, instruments are always given opportunities to express their individual personality, and yet at other times certain combinations of instruments absolutely require the broad-range middle-ground character of the *sheng* to provide the ensemble with its characteristic ensemble sound, and the orchestra with its characteristic orchestra sound. The roles of these wind instruments are unfamiliar to modern Western composers. I specially used the term modern Western composers because It is not clear whether in historical times Western musicians had not been in contact with this type of orchestration. In fact judging from the flow of resonator design across the Asian-European continent, it is almost certain that many of the Chinese instruments and their use in ensemble practice, a very old practice, were witnessed by Westerners. But because of the difficulties in long-distance travel, only parts of individual instrument performance and acoustical design were transferred. The broader art and science of ensemble and orchestral practices were lost.

The mid-range *suona* today popular in Chinese orchestras is an instrument with a special potential. It is a natural double-reed which is not as constrained as the oboe, and yet a good oboe player can probably pick up its techniques in a short time. To play it like a true *suona*, however, requires complete familiarity with Chinese *shengguan* music. The mid-range *suona*, unlike the *guanzi* at the far end of the *shengguan* spectrum, has its very mellow range. At the same time at the high and at the low ranges, it is capable of the most interesting improvisational sounds. Jazz musicians who have played it want to find all the *suona* in the world. Here I recall many conversations with Phil Cohran. Its acoustical efficiency is also quite a bit higher than the oboe. Its reed is detachable from the mouth piece, so that one can quickly change the style of reed to turn it into a whole new instrument.

Today we reexamine the topic from a practical point of view, of utilizing our understanding in ensemble art and ensemble acoustics. We reviewed the parallel use of melodic and harmonic instruments in the *shengguan* group. We examines the complete system of acoustical resonators that shape *guanyue* today. We further looked at the possibilities of the *shengguan* group as orchestral tonal basis from the standpoint of Shen, 1989. We discover the usefulness of appreciating the philosophical foundation of the *shengguan* group. This *shengguan* group is acoustically, technically and tonal spectrum-wise the broadest wind instrument combination anywhere. And the *guanyue* family, the Chinese winds, offer acoustical, technical, and aesthetic possibilities today to Western musicians and composers which were not available or not accessible in the past.

REFERENCES

Baines, Anthony, Woodwind Instruments and Their History, Dover, New York (1991).

CMSNA, Exhibition on the Music of the Chinese Orchestra, *Chinese Music*, **3**, 60 (1980).

Creel, Herlee Glessner, *The Birth of China*, Ungar, New York (1937).

Hayashi Kenzo, *Dongya Yueqi Kao* (Study of East Asian Instruments, in Chinese), Yinyue Chubanshe, Beijing (1962).

Henan Province Research Institute of Cultural Relics, Henan Wuyang Jiahu Xinshiqi Shidai Yizhi Di Er Zhi Liu Ci Fajue Jianbao (Brief Report of the Excavation of the Neolithic Sites at Jiahu in Wuyang County of Henan :1st-6th Seasons, in Chinese), *Wenwu*, 1989 Issue Number 1 (1989), 1.

Huang Xiang-peng, Wuyang Jiahu Gudi De Ceyin Yanjiu (Pitch Measurement Studies of Bone Flutes from Jiahu of Wuyang County, in Chinese), *Wenwu*, 1989 Issue Number 1 (1989), 15.

Joppig, Gunther, *The Oboe and the Bassoon*, Amadeus Press, Portland Oregon (1988).

Lee Yuan-Yuan, An Amazing Discovery in Chinese Music, *Chinese Music*, **2**, 16 (1979).

Reeded Winds

Lee Yuan-Yuan, Follow-up on "An Amazing Discovery in Chinese Music", *Chinese Music*, **2**, 39 (1979).

Lee Yuan-Yuan, The Music of the Zenghou Zhong, *Chinese Music*, **3**, 3 (1980).

Meylan, Raymond, *The Flute*, Amadeus Press, Portland Oregon (1988).

Needham, Joseph, *Science and Civilization in China*, Volume 4: Physics and Physical Technology, Cambridge (1962).

Qu Guang-yi, Woguo Xinshiqi Shidai De Zhuzhi Dilei Yueqi Tuiyi, *Yueqi*, 1989, No. 1, 7 (1989).

Shen, Sin-yan, Acoustics of Ancient Chinese Bells, *Scientific American*, **255**, No. 4, 104 (1987).

Shen, Sin-yan, What Makes Chinese Music Chinese? *Chinese Music*, **4**, 23 (1981).

Shen, Sin-yan, Gamle Kinesiske Klokkers Akustik (in Danish), *Acta Campanologica*, **4**, 141 (1989).

Shen, Sin-yan, Instruments of the Chinese Orchestra, *Chinese Music*, **7**, 33 (1984).

Shen, Sin-yan, Acoustics of Ancient Chinese Bells (in Japanese), *Scientific American* (Tokyo), **17**, 104 (1987).

Shen, Sin-yan, Foundations of the Chinese Orchestra, *Chinese Music*, **2**, 32 (1979).

Shen, Sin-yan, Zhongguo Yinyuejie Dui Renlei Ying Fu De Zeren (in Chinese), *Zhongguo Yinyue*, 1982, No. 2, 18 (1982).

Shen, Sin-yan, The Shanghai Traditional Orchestra and He Wu-qi, *Chinese Music*, **5**, 43 (1982).

Shen, Sin-yan, Foundations of the Chinese Orchestra II, *Chinese Music,* **3**, 16 (1980).

Shen, Sin-yan, On the Acoustical Space of the Chinese Orchestra (in Chinese), *People's Music,* 1989, No. 2, 2 (1989).

Shen, Sin-yan, On the System of Chinese Fiddles I, *Chinese Music,* **13**, 24 (1990).

Shen, Sin-yan, On the System of Chinese Fiddles II, *Chinese Music,* **13**, 44 (1990).

University of California at San Diego Arts & Lectures, Program Notes by Shen Sin-yan for the Silk and Bamboo Ensemble, March 9, 1990 (1990).

Wang Tiechui, The Music of the Chuigehui Orchestra at the Ziwei Village of Ding County, Part I, *Chinese Music,* **10**, 23 (1987); Part II, *Chinese Music,* **10**, 43 (1987).

Wenhuabu Wenxue Yishu Yanjiushuo Yinyue Wudao Yanjiushi, *Zhongguo Yueqi Jieshao,* Renmin Yinyue Chubanshe, Beijing (1978).

Yue Sheng, *Minzu Yueqi Zhizuo Gaishu,* Qinggongye Chubanshe, Beijing (1980).

Zhao Licheng and Shen Sin-yan, The Music of the Suona, *Chinese Music,* **11**, 23 (1988).

■

Qin: Timeless Music

While scores are written by musicians of instrumental and vocal music, the rhythmic elements and tempo are considered the last items of importance, in order not to constrain performance. This concept made classical Chinese compositions timeless and easily adaptable to changes in musical taste, which as we now well know is a strong function of time and period. The result is the successful propagation of compositions through time, making them therefore truly timeless. This is the case of the instrumental school of the *qin* and the vocal school of the *qin-ge* (the *qin* songs). The horizontal zither *qin* is an important historical instrument and has associated with it a very large number of known compositions passed down through history. Its methods of notation is based on the concept of timeless music. Yet at the same time the *true character* of the music and the player, as in the requirements of changes in tonal quality, is very much emphasized throughout.

Music that is truly timeless has been the dream of composers throughout the ages. In this paper we discuss the rhythmic philosophy - a timeless philosophy - that exists in

Chinese Musical Instruments

CHINESE CLASSICAL MUSIC IS TIMELESS: the rhythmic elements and tempo are considered the last items of importance, in order not to constrain performance. This concept made classical Chinese compositions easily adaptable to changes in musical taste of rhythm amd metering, which are strong functions of time period. The result is the successful propagation of a large number of the best compositions through time, making them therefore truly timeless.

Chinese classical music. The metering of Chinese music is difficult and we will discuss why that is the case. While scores are written down by musicians for both instrumental and vocal music, the rhythmic elements and tempo are considered the last items of importance, in order not to constrain performance. This concept made classical compositions timeless and easily adaptable to changes in musical taste, which is a strong function of time, as a result of which these compositions are passed on successfully through time, and are therefore truly timeless. We analyze the changes in that philosophy during different periods, and the recent neglect of it in the 20th century.

THE RHYTHMIC PHILOSOPHY OF CHINESE CLASSICAL MUSIC

The breadth of rhythmic concepts is often a focus of attention during concerts, pre-concerts, as well as post-concert discussions during the tours of the Silk & Bamboo Ensemble and the Chinese Classical Orchestra in the 1970s, the 1980s and the 1990s. Compared with popular music or classical music in the United States, the musical performance at concert programs of the above groups has been said to offer "an astonishing range of rhythmic variations" by critics who are usually comparing the performance they just experienced with other performances that they are familiar with, usually Western classical or popular. The basis of the comparison is a musical experience truly engaging and fascinating. To look at the comparison closely, however, one may encounter the age-old questions of "What really makes interesting music?" and "How do we compose successful music?" Were those both practical as well as philosophical questions on the minds of the great Chinese classical composers? I imagine they were to a limited extent. But apparently more on their mind was the question of where we fit as a human race in the grand scheme of the universe, and in space and in time. Those thoughts led to the way Chinese classical music was written and the way they were passed on as we've come to know them now.

SPACE AND TIME

That was certainly the case for a long time, before the Song period. Music of Tang (618-907) and before was distinctly different from music afterwards due to one very important point: the perspectives of the musician and the composer. Ancient music through the Tang period was *cosmic* in perspective. Celestial bodies and their relation to earth and to humans occupy a large part of the experience of man's very own existence among the cosmos. Man's coexistence with natural forces formed a large part of where musicians thought they stood. The study of musical acoustics flourished. After Tang, however, man became different, and significantly more concerned about his immediate human environment, and his own individual thoughts. Was there an advancement or a decline in the philosophy of life? We can probably look at it two ways. The music before Tang and through the powerful part of Tang (Tang established global political and military power and remained powerful until towards the end) gave a sense of destiny and pride, in terms of understanding of the position of the human race, where civilization really fitted, where it could make the most contribution universally, and where the highest interests of life could be found - e.g. in the mathematical and acoustical arena of sound and music. In the music after Tang we found musicians not only to return to the description of ancient sufferings that occupy everyday life, but also to amplify the emotions and thoughts associated with personal problems and social problems. Music reflects social progress and social change; The entrance of the Song period (960-1279) is thus the beginning of a politically

weak period in Chinese history, globally speaking. Philosophy
and aesthetics deteriorated in this time period, and so did music.
Folk music, however, flourished in the silk and bamboo school
and in the reed and percussion school, focusing more on
acoustical effects of the ensembles, a new accomplishment that
was more independent of the content of the titles of music.

Many westerner scholars and musicians who studied
Chinese music at the turn of the 20th century encountered a
large number of problems in transcribing Chinese music. A
frequent problem was of course associated with the
"embellishments" and the "nuances", that varied distinctly from
performer to performer, and from one performance environment
to another. Strictly speaking, these situations were not to be
called "performances" because despite the fact that audience
existed the players "played", and allowed their emotional
priorities to take charge as they "jammed" for their own musical
benefit and thus "did not perform" with the intention of satisfying
their audience's musical expectations. Then came the larger
problem of reading the scores. So frequently western scholars and
researchers were astonished to find no tempo or meter was
indicated. During performances, complex patterns of pitch and
interval usage and instrumental acoustics were apparent but were
going too fast for a proper digestion (Yang, 1984). *Qin* students
who studied the *qin* scores faced the same problem (In fact many
researchers would settle for interpreted scores with timing and
rhythm written in, see e.g. Xihu Qinshe, 1993). Much confusion
was attributed to difficulties with cadences but little attention
was paid to the true cause of the problem: a different perspective

with respect to the "Rhythmic Philosophy" that is present in Chinese classical music.

This can be understood today by looking at how music changes with time, and, in fact, the possible thinking of the Chinese masters, who notated their music as scores, in deciding what to put down and what not to put down, in order to make good music immortal and allow the creative process to be forever present whenever music is made.

Let us look at the evolution of music throughout the ages. Several types of changes reflected in the change of times. The sound, the instrumentation, whether we liked reedy sounds, whether we liked dynamically contrasting sounds, and whether we liked more subtle musical flow contributes to one area of musical psychology. The main area of change through the ages could be found, however, in rhythm and meter. A song, or an instrumental piece, at different times in history would acquire different rhythmic treatment. But the main musical material, the

Ex. 1   [1]   ♩=48→

Ex. 2

Ex. 3

interval contrast in the melody and the harmony, would remind us that the same piece of music is being played. The Chinese masters caught this concept and used it to the fullest extent.

The interpretation of *qin* music is an art that makes music timeless. Pitches, intervals, and important changes in tones are all specified, but no meter or rhythm is usually stated to constrain

Ex. 4

the player. This was the case for a long time until more recent
scores such as Wang Yanqing's scores from Shandong which had
such constrains.

The concepts here refer to the "timelessness" of classical
compositions. Look at "The Orchid in Seclusion" (Youlan) which
has been interpreted countless number of times by today's artists.
Let's look at some versions (See Zhongguo Yishu Yanjiuyuan
Yinyue Yanjiushuo and Beijing Guqin Society, 1982, Zhongguo
Yishu Yanjiuyuan Yinyue Yanjiushuo and Beijing Guqin Society,
1983, and Zhongyang Yinyue Xueyuan Zhongguo Yinyue
Yanjiushuo and Beijing Guqin Society, 1963). Ex. 1 is from Guan
Pinghu. Ex. 2 is from Wu Zhengping. Ex. 3 is from Xu Lisun,
and Ex. 4 is from Yao Bingyan.

When Kong Zi, Confucius, traveled to all the main
principalities in China and found himself not seriously considered
by any, thoughts began to emerge. On his way back to the
principality of Lu, today's Shandong Province, he found the

fragrant orchid among weeds, and found himself in similar situations. He sang on the *qin* these thoughts. According to what we know today, there are more than thirty versions of this music, all instrumental without word. Some contained a single movement, some three, some eight, and some more than ten. The above, however, were all interpretations of Ex. 5.

Ex. 5

那臥中指十上半寸許素商食指中指雙拏宮商中

指急下与构俱下十三下一寸許住末商起食指散緩半

扶宮商食指桃起又半扶宮商縱容下無名扲十三外一

寸許案面角即作兩半扶挑聲一句緩緩起

中指當十竪素商緩緩散歷羽徵無名打商食指桃徵

一句大指當八案面無名打商食指散桃羽無名當十一

素宮無名打宮徵吟一句大指當九案宮商疾全扶宮

商抄大指當八案商無名打商大指徐徐抑上八上一寸

許急末取聲散打宮無名當十案徵食指桃徵應一句

無名不動下大指當九案徵做羽卻轉徵羽食指節過

徵大指急蹴徵上至八挑徵起無名不動無名散打宮

食指桃徵應一句無名不動又下大指當九案徵羽急全扶徵

打宮桃徵大指挑徵起大指還當九案徵羽急全扶徵

羽舉大指屈無名當九十間案文武食指打文下大

97

Metering of Chinese music is difficult. Western musicians who study silk and bamboo music today are often fooled by the metering indicated by the simplified published scores. When studied in detail, the performances bear no resemblance to these scores. And here I am not referring to the oversimplification of the score as to the pitches performed and the lack of notations for embellishments. The worst situation is encountered when the scores lied - the accentuations do not fall where they are supposed to be according to western conventions, i.e. the strong beat did not occur at the beginning of the bar. In actual fact, Chinese music is best not metered. Phrasing and breathing marks do work, however. In fact these are so much more honest and reliable if you pay attention only to them, and pay no attention to the bars. Traditional Chinese musicians don't look at the bars.

Today's popular music overemphasizes pulses and beats, to such an extent that many young musicians will have trouble with a piece of music when they can not clearly sense the pulses and the beats. But in actual fact, in the current overemphasis of pulses and beats, sensitivity towards metering and time is totally lost. Only well known and popular accentuation patterns are kept, and many new age composers are therefore trapped.

Bear in mind what we are talking about here is performance and composition as the creative processes of music making. When we become uncreative in any one aspect of what music really is, we are in deep trouble. That is the problem with a lot of the commercial music today.

In Chinese music, the allocation of time and apportioning of space is decided by the amount of thinking involved and the appropriate distribution of weight.

The weight in terms of length in time and forcefulness in dynamics are measured according to the performers' perception and not according to that of the composer. This is best illustrated by such pieces as "Listen to the pine", "Wedding Processional", and many others.

We hear nowadays frequently recordings by music school graduates in China who could only go by the score, and the recordings of these pieces are absolutely terrible in the sense that no music or genuine interest could be found in the performance. Many music critics who heard these recordings have told me that these recordings sounded like background music or studies.

When true artists like the Shanghai Traditional Orchestra of the 1950s played "Wedding Processional", the musical interest was immeasurable, primarily because true music came out of the creative and collaborative music making process of musicians who ignored the "standards" of the score.

THE MUSIC MAKING PROCESS AND THE ROLE OF THE SCORE

The horizontal zither *qin* is not a popular instrument today. It however is an important historical instrument and has associated with it a very large number of known compositions. Its methods of notation provide food for thought on the subject of timeless music. The method of notation of *qin* music has been widely studied. In particular, the manner in which master players recreate (the recreation process is known as *dapu*) the music according to their interpretation of the score (*pu*) reflects significantly the manner in which the Chinese people treat music. The tempo and speed in which a composition is played upon *dapu* interpretation can vary drastically between master players, yet everyone knows the same piece is being played when they listen to the different renditions. This phenomenon offers spheres of expanded thoughts for composers today.

Frequently in western music, we find musicians paying a lot of attention to the score, sometimes with so much attention that the creativity of the music making process is overlooked. As we all know, preference for tempo and rhythm are strong functions of time period. Putting too much emphasis on these aspects of a music can seriously impede musical development. I will illustrate why this is the case. When Whitney Houston sings a song that had earlier been sung by Dolly Parton, the rhythmic element of the song is totally modified, giving the song a totally new life. And yet it is really the same song sung in a different style, and in this case reflecting preferences of this new time period. Such adaptation processes do not occur as frequently in classical music today. The *dapu* process of musical thinking for the *qin* offer new dimensions for advancements in classical music composition. The *qin* masters over the ages wrote their pieces anticipating changes in rhythmic and other preferences in music making, thus making their music new and lively at all times, in turn making their music timeless.

This philosophy, however, is not well understood by many Chinese musicians today. As a result of miscommunication and misunderstanding, *qin* music has been looked upon only with historical relevance and little musical enthusiasm, in many cases.

THE QIN

The *qin* is a Chinese plucked string instrument with elongated trapezoidal and slightly arched wooden box resonator and seven strings but no bridges. The strings are plucked by the right-hand fingers while the left hand fingers stops the strings at desired lengths. Thirteen small ivory or mother-of-pearl disks inlaid in the resonator surface provide reference for the stopping points and positions of harmonics. Over two-hundred notations are used to indicate the playing technique, stopping position, and tonal requirements. The use of harmonics in melodic progression is a characteristic feature of compositions. A total of ninety-one choices is available. The open strings, the stopped pitches and the harmonics are used in contrast with each other. A very large repertory exists for this instrument and best known players include Si Kuang, Si Wen, Si Xiang (Spring and Autumn and the Warring States Period, 770 BC - 221 BC), Cai Wen-ji (177 AD - ?, Han Period), Ji Kang (227 - 263 AD, Jin Period), Guo Chu-wang (1190 - 1260, Song Period, Wang Yan-qing (1866 - 1921), Guan Pinghu (1887 - 1967), Xu Yuanbai (1893 - 1957), Zha Fuxi (1895 - 1976), Wu Jinglue (1906-) and others. Recent masters who cover many schools include Gong Yi.

The body of the *qin* consists of head, body, and end parts. The ancients considered the *qin* to have head, waist, and back.

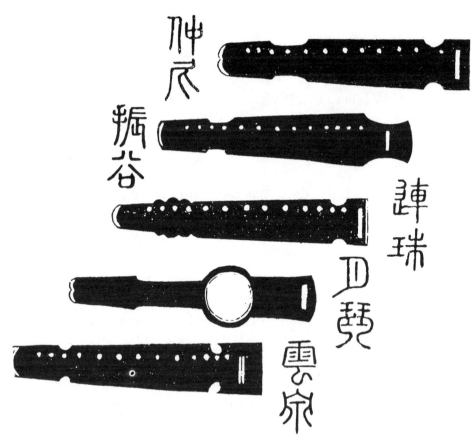

They went as far as calling these parts the golden boy head, the jade maiden waist, and the fairy back. Its various components are also named in terms of the dragon, the phoenix, gold, and jade. The ancients designed the *qin* to be 3 feet 6 inches and 5 minutes in Chinese lengths. It signified that one revolution in heaven was three hundred and sixty five degrees and a year consisted of three hundred and sixty five days. The *qin* has upper and lower surfaces, connoting the interaction of heaven and earth. There are thirteen "*hui*" markings for performing harmonics, signifying the twelve months in a year plus a leap-year month.

There is systematic difference between the *qin* and most other string instruments of the world. Most string instruments such as the violin use a narrow area for fingering (such as the fingerboard of the violin). The *qin* uses its complete surface for fingering. Most string instruments have pegs (for tuning strings) located on the upper left. The *qin* has all pegs located at the lower right. Apart from the *konghou* (harp) which has severe shape restriction, all string instruments have lowest string located near the player's body. All strings on the *qin* have the same length, producing no shape restriction for the *qin*. The *qin* however has lowest string located on the outer side, with respect to the player. Many string instruments have sound holes on the front surface, and the *qin* has sound holes on the back.

The *qin* master Zha Fu-xi once said that "some music historians tend to consider string instruments of the Asia-Europe continent to be of one origin because most string instruments are of similar constructions. But the case of the *qin* is opposite to all common construction of string instruments. Does it have a different origin on the banks of the Yangzi and the Yellow Rivers which possibly had its own ancient system of musical culture? Recent discoveries in Chu culture illuminate this point. The *qin* today appear to be connected to the Chu and Han string family. Xu Shen's interpretation of the form of *qin* in ideograph appears incorrect".

Qin and *se* are popular string instruments of ancient China. The *se* has movable bridges and the *qin* has none. Their number of strings also varies quite a bit from period to period and from region to region. Both instruments were frequent musical partners for a long time in history. The musical treasures of Zenghou Yi in Hubei, for example, contain many such string instruments in the orchestras (see e.g. Lee, in *Chinese Music*, several issues in 1979). The seven string version of the *qin* now used was popular during the Han period more than two thousand years ago. *Qin* artists including Shi Zhong, Zhao Ding, Long De and others were known in history. It was also absorbed into the royal court. The famous *qin* artist Ji Kang lived at the end of the Han period. One of the earliest *qin* score has been handed down by a folk artist Qiu Ming (500-590).

Chinese artists who played the *qin* during the Six Dynasties period expanded upon the repertoire of the Chu and Han culture. When the Tang period came, great artists such as Zhao Ye-li, Dong Ting-lan, Chen Kang-shi and others assimilated other music including the Zhu school of music (Zhu-jia Sheng) and the Shen school of music (Shen-jia Sheng), boldly created large numbers of compositions and theoretical treaties. Unfortunately due to the shortsightedness of the elite class to follow, much of this treasure was lost.

In the weak Song period, many scholars played the *qin*, but good compositions were few (See Zhongguo Yinyuejia Xiehui, 1960). From historical documents remaining, we know of *qin* artists including Sun Dao-zi and Zeng Yi-hai. The scholar Fan Zhong-yan is known to play the *qin* well. Ouyang Xiu frequently discussed the aesthetics of the *qin*. Su Dong-po not only played the *qin*, but also composed. He recognized that *qin* music "was the sound of Zheng and Wei", meaning it came from folk music. Two small compositions of this period "Gu Yuan" and "Huangying Yin" can not be compared to compositions before Song. But at the time that Song was defeated, numerous *qin* artists emerged with great artistry and social outlook. Guo Chu-wang of this time period who lived from the Song to the Yuan period composed the masterpiece "Xiao Xiang Shui-yun" (Mist Over the Xiao and Xiang Rivers). Mao Ming-zhong composed the colorful masterpiece "Qiao Ge" which had its origin in Chu music. Wang Da-you composed for Wen Tian-xiang in jail the suite of "Ju You". They are such tremendous compositions that they are passed down to us.

THE RECENT NEGLECTS

Timeless music has been a unique and profound philosophy of the Chinese musicians. Unfortunately, timelessness has not been on the mind of the music community in recent decades. It has been neglected. Late nineteenth century and early twentieth century Chinese music was in one of the poorest shapes in Chinese history. Little effort on the part of the Chinese society was put into music. During the war years of the Sino-Japanese war, vocal and choral music were composed for important reasons, and they played a most positive role in increasing the will of the Chinese people in the war. Music as a whole was economically and socially revived after 1949 and professional musicianship became supported at a very high level by the Chinese government. The timelessness philosophy of Chinese music was, however, not recognized nor studied in the music schools, except perhaps on an individual basis. Much of the success in this recent period centered on the collection of folk music, and the revival of folk traditions. On the professional performance front, the composition and arrangements of this period were not entirely healthy. Following the west, rhythm and tempo became the more important elements. The Chinese, during this period, started almost from scratch philosophically. Substantial effort was put in to "modernize" and follow the blip in western music's historical development of emphasizing the importance of atonal compositions. These efforts of "tide riding" proved unfruitful. Today, we have produced a large number of music students who are skilled in western composition styles, and western aesthetics in orchestration and acoustics, but have paid little attention to their own "timeless" musical philosophy. This is similar to the neglect of the generalized "harmony" philosophy in (see e.g. Shen, 1991) Chinese classical music - music schools went after specialized but restricted harmonic concepts from the west and dumped the grand generalized harmonic framework present in Chinese music.

The purpose of this writing is to alert the music community both in China and in the west that: (1) the music that we hear on a day to day basis in China is possibly not very Chinese or unique, (2) it is time that China and the world look seriously at the "timeless" perspective of musical composition which was for a very long time a powerful tradition that sustained music development, in the only civilization that prospered in music without interruptions despite drastic political changes domestically and globally.

REFERENCES

Lee Yuan-Yuan, in *Chinese Music*, **2**, numerous issues (1979).

Shen Sin-yan, *Chinese Music and Orchestration: A Primer on Principles and Practice*, Chinese Music Society of North America, Chicago (1991).

Xihu Qinshe (West Lake Qin Society), *Xu Yuanbai Danchen Yibai Zhounian Jinianche* (100th Anniversary of Xu Yuanbai's Birth, in Chinese), Xihu Qinshe, Hangzhou (1993).

Yang Yin-liu, A Bewildered Western Musician, *Chinese Music*, **7**, 4 (1984).

Zhongguo Yinyuejia Xiehui (All China Musician's Association), *Yinyue Jianshe Wenji* (Collection of Essays on Musical Construction, in Chinese), Music Press, Beijing (1960).

Zhongguo Yishu Yanjiuyuan (Chinese Academy of the Arts) Yinyue Yanjiushuo (Music Research Institute) and Beijing Guqin Society, *Guqin Quji* (Collection of Guqin Music, in Chinese), People's Music Press, Beijing (1982).

Zhongguo Yishu Yanjiuyuan (Chinese Academy of the Arts) Yinyue Yanjiushuo (Music Research Institute) and Beijing Guqin Society, *Guqin Quji* (Collection of Guqin Music, in Chinese), Vol. 2, People's Music Press, Beijing (1983).

Zhongyang Yinyue Xueyuan (Central Conservatory of Music) Zhongguo Yinyue Yanjiushuo (Chinese Music Research Institute) and Beijing Guqin Society, *Guqin Jicheng* (Anthology of Guqin Music, in Chinese), Vol. 1, First Half, Zhonghua Press, Beijing (1963).

■

Fingerboard & Fretted Lutes:
Xianzi & Pipa

SANXIAN: FINGERBOARD LUTE

Fretted and fingerboard lutes in Chinese music are some of the most intriguing plucked instruments in the world. Whenever we think about the timbres of the plucked string, the *ud* and the *guitar* come immediately to mind. The *ud* is still a popular classical instrument in the Twin Rivers region today, and the *guitar* is the most popular modern lute anywhere. What is less known to the outside world are the highly developed *sanxian* and *pipa* in Chinese music. To us, they are passionately known as the *xianzi* and the *pipa*.

Fretted and fingerboard lutes developed side by side in China and they are loved for their drastically different timbre. The *sanxian*, also called *xianzi*, is my favorite lute in that its performance art is completely free in the use of the fingerboard. All Chinese lutes pride right hand fingering techniques - thus the use of a pick or plectrum would not be considered the highest form of artistry. Performance of the *sanxian* requires total physiological freedom. You get any tone around any pitch pattern you want by using the most appropriate left and right hand coordination. Such is the personality of this fabulous instrument. Its acoustics is characterized by resonant rolls and chords that are very powerful, and by the sound of large glissando slides on the fingerboard with the whole left hand. Ths *sanxian*, especially the smaller versions, is an important component of the silk and bamboo ensemble (University of California, 1990).

The *sanxian* is a drum guitar. Its resonator is called a drum and is physically a drum. It came from the category of "*tantiao* instruments" (see Shen, 1981a) which uses strings whose lengths extend much beyond that of the resonator. Here I refer to the contrast between the category of *qins* (*qin, se, zheng, yangqin*) which have strings the length of their resonators, and the category of *pipas* (*ruan, hulei, pipa, liuqin, sanxian*) which have strings much longer than the effective acoustical length of their resonators. While we review the 20th Century, we observe in China the tendency to unify the sounds of the many different Chinese orchestras, and in so doing the *sanxian* is almost completely lost. In particular we no longer see the *xiaosanxian* (the higher pitched and older version) at all on scores. The *xiaosanxian* is an absolute gem in providing Jiangnan-styled cultural acoustics found most prevalently in the Shanghai area. It is a major regional instrument even in the 20th Century. However it is somewhat neglected in the music school system, and completely neglected by professional orchestral composers. Even the large *sanxian* is most frequently used only as a color instrument among the works of the younger composers. What a shame!

SANXIAN ACOUSTICS is characterized by resonant rolls and powerful chords. Left hand positions cover the *whole length* of the fingerboard post - the sound of *large glissando slides* on the fingerboard being prevalent.

Musicologists often traced the *sanxian* back to the days of the *qinhanzi* 2000 years ago (see Cao, 1957, Chang, 1957). The *hulei* was actually a popular fingerboard lute before the present-day *sanxian*. In the Tang courts musical instrument makers made varieties of *hulei* which have today become cultural relics. The idea of the *hulei* and the *sanxian* were acoustically very similar - a membrane drum resonator was used to support fretless artistry on the left hand. Here I must emphasize the "fretless" part of the performance art on the *sanxian*. On the *sanxian* - because of its size and length of strings - very large open-string resonance can be heard throughout its range. Large glissando is also the result of

110

THE *HULEI* was made popular in the Tang period. Zheng Zhongcheng of the Emporor Wenzong period (827-840) excelled in the large and the small *hulei*. The *hulei* has a pear-shaped python-skin drum resonator, a medium-length fingerboard, and a dragon head. The famous Tang painter Han Huang was a well known maker of this instrument.

this construction and thus its musical requirement. Another instrument in this family is the Mongolian *huobusi* (Wang, 1931, Jia, 1981), but it has a much narrower performance capability compared with the *sanxian*. In more recent times, the *sanxian* design has also been used in the construction of fiddles (bowed) such as in the case of the *zhuihu*, the *zhuiqin*, and the *leiqin*.

The *sanxian* has three strings, tuned according to the universal system of fourth-fifth or fifth-fourth stacking (This is true today of the liuqin small lute and the ruan round lute family). Today the name *sanxian* refers to the complete group of long-necked, fretless Chinese lutes with three strings, a rectangular resonator with python skin front and back, and a curved-back pegbox with side pegs. The Japanese version is a close cousin. The instrument is popular in theatrical accompaniment, ballad-singing accompaniment, and in the orchestra. The large *sanxian* is about 1.2 meters long and the small *sanxian* is about 0.96 meters long. Common tuning of the large *sanxian* is between D, A, d and G, d, g, and that of the

THE SANXIAN IS THE PRINCIPAL LUTE in this Ming illustration (left) of a silk & bamboo musical gathering (The artist apparently was not entirely familiar with musical instruments - details of the performing methods and sizes of some instruments may thus be in error).

small is between A, d, a, and d, a, d' (top note just above middle C). It has a compass of three octaves and is played with fingernails of the right hand. Its performance is characterized by powerful resonant rolls and chords, as well as large glissandos on the fingerboard. In recent times, Bai Feng-yan (1899 - 1975), Li Yi, Zhou Run-ming and others gave the *sanxian* increased importance as a solo instrument. He Wu-qi (see Shen, 1982), Peng Xiu-wen (see Shen, 1996a and Shen, 1996b), and Zhu Jian-Er used the large *sanxian* prominently in a number of classic compositions for the Chinese orchestra. The role of the *sanxian* in the Chinese orchestra was featured in a number of prominent CMSNA Exhibition in the United States (see e.g. CMSNA, 1980).

The *sanxian* and the *pipa* are principal members of the Chinese orchestra (for their specific roles in contrast with other instruments see Shen, 1979, Shen, 1980). Chinese orchestration is based on the use of *si* (silk), *zhu* (bamboo), *chui* (reeded wind) and *da* (percussion) tonal components, and tonal interest presides over melodic or harmonic interest in orchestral interpretations. The masterly and meticulous use of tonal interest is evident throughout Chinese instrumental repertoire. In contrast with a Western string quartet which consists of all fiddles, the Chinese string quartet has a plucked base. The xiansuo string quartet, for example, uses a *huqin* fiddle (to provide bowed sound), a *zheng*

THE MOON ON HIGH showcases a fiddle, a pipa, a sanxian (xianzi), and the zheng. This northern "xiansuo" string ensemble sometimes also feature other additional instruments.

horizontal open-stringed wooden zither and two plucked lutes of different timbre (a *pipa* which is fretted and wooden with a rounded back and the other finger-boarded with a python-skin resonator, the *sanxian*). The spectrum of musical effects resulting from the available timbre and playing techniques provides an endless source of musical interest in such a combination. The full score from the *xiansuo* quartet "The Moon on High" showcases a fiddle, a *pipa*, a *xianzi* (the *sanxian*), and the *zheng*, in their strictly instrumental roles (see beginning of first movement left). This northern string ensemble sometimes also feature other additional instruments (see Ng, 1980, Exhibition, 1980).

PIPA & RUAN

Compared with the *sanxian*, the *pipa* has not been my favorite instrument because of its 20th Century repertory. The *pipa* is a highly developed instrument in that it commands a large repertory that is strictly speaking purely instrumental. Perhaps because of the popularization of the *pipa* as a song and dance instrument in the second half of the 20th Century, there appeared a significant number of compositions which over-emphasized the *changlun* long rolling strum which has a highly expressive singing quality. Thus folk songs are converted into *pipa* solo. Orchestral practices become confused in which the singing quality of the pipa group is often the main thing emphasized. I support Li Tingsong who once said that the *pipa* is such an instrument that you can get any temperament system out of its frets - he was, of course, talking about general pipa artistry in which the masters combined just intervals with artistic intervals in left-hand expressions. The *pipa* is fact is such a high-class instrument that it is in the league of the *qin* - the scholarly musical instrument which is the master instrument on which to manipulate pure instrumental tones. Such appreciation for the *pipa* is apparanetly lost in second half of the 20th Century. We see two things happening to the *pipa*: it is used to play chords,

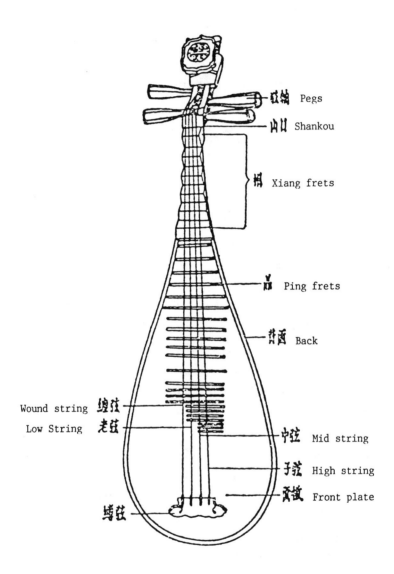

THE *PIPA* WAS A DESCENDENT OF THE *RUAN.* Historically *pipa* artists and instrument makers combined the pear-shaped resonator and the fret-fingering and right-hand "tantiao" techniques of the ancient *ruan* (right).

VIVID RIGHT-HAND ARTISTRY ON THE *RUAN* is clearly shown by this artist. This painting is a Song copy of the master work of Zhou Wen-ju of the Five Dynasty. The *ruan* is the oldest lute on which present-day high level of right-hand lute techniques were developed.

and the *pipa* is used to play melodic passages. These constrain the broad and truly instrumental applications of *pipa* acoustics. These are also rather simplistic uses of this marvelous instrument. We have had many discussions on this topic with 20th Century composers. I hope things will be quite different in the 21st Century and beyond!

The broad range of classical compositions for the *pipa* remain today the treasures of Chinese music. "Yuer Gao" (The Moon on High) and "Sai Shang Qu" (Song North of the Border) are all time favorites, and have been recorded solo and with orchestra by numerous artists (See e.g. Shen, 1998). In the 1950s Li Tingsong, originally of Suzhou, recorded some of the most wonderful classics in instrumental *pipa* repertory. They included "Bawang Xiejia", "Qinglian Yuefu", "Xiyang Xiaogu", "Shimian Maifu", "Dengyue Jiaohui" and others. Li's recordings exemplify what he preaches, which is that all three temperament systems are used in conjunction on the *pipa* -

a fact known to very few. After Li, few *pipa* players understood
this joint-temperament system in Chinese plucked strings, and
most younger players moved towards equal temperament. This is
a common trend in most Chinese instruments. But for the *pipa*,
we were fortunate to have a transitional master Li Tingsong. It
indeed is amazing that the ear of modern society has become so
unskilled that we have now been trained to reject musically just
intervals! This brings back our discussions on cultural acoustics.
We might say that modern society with its commercial culture
has produced a highly simplistic cultural acoustics.

The name *pipa* now refers to a large class of Chinese
plucked lutes. The common version that we usually talk about
has a short neck, a pear-shaped body with a wooden belly.
There are six convex frets on the neck and 23 frets on the belly.
The four strings run from a fastener on the belly to conical
tuning pegs in the sides of the bent-back pegbox. They are
plucked with all five fingers of the right-hand while the
instrument is held vertically on the thigh. It is present in most
regional orchestras and is an important solo instrument with a
large repertory. Its performance is characterized by repeated
strumming utilizing fingers in a continuous roll, producing an
undulating long-tremolo, and chords made up of fourths, fifths
and thirds. A common tuning is a-d-e-a' (top note below middle
C). This tuning follows the harmonic skeleton of Chinese cultural
acoustics (for these harmonic structures see Shen, 1981b).

Another version of the *pipa*, more ancient, has a round
belly and a long neck and is known as the *ruan*, with four
common sizes. The *ruan* was the *pipa*-family instrument on

which the right-rand techniques of the *pipa* was developed historically. The *zhongruan* (the mid-ranged) and the *daruan* (the low-ranged) are today used to complement the *pipa*, the *sanxian*, the *liuqin* (the high lute), and the *yangqin* (the harmonizing hammered dulcimer of the Chinese orchestra) in the plucked-string section of the Chinese orchestra. This whole *ruan* group (above) has the fabulous acoustics of <u>thick resonant vibrating strings</u> when played using fingers. When a plectrum is used, however, the *ruan* acoustics is altered to reflect more of an empty-box sound. I call your attention to the *zhongruan* performance of Zhang Xinghua of the Central Traditional orchestra. He makes the *ruan* sound like a low wind instrument, extremely tantalizing. Zhang's finger techniques represent some of the highest in the history of the *ruan*. This more ancient style of performance is far more superior musically than the guitar-like performances

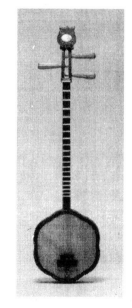

QINQIN, a cousin of the *ruan,* is popular in Southern China.

119

Ode to Meihua (*Nanyue* Southern Music)

I.   Snow in Early Spring

Notation According to Liu Honggou

which is often seen today. In southern music, the *qinqin*, a cousin of the *ruan*, is frequently used.

The *xianzi* and the *pipa* are old partners in *nanyin* Southern music. The large suite "Meihua Chao" (Ode to Meihua) of Fujian begins with "Snow in Early Spring" (above), which features the *xianzi* and the *pipa* as the first part, and the *dongxiao* and the *erxian* as the second part. Here the musical intent is to have the *tantiao* effects (which is highly percussive) of the *sanxian* and *pipa* strings complemented by the lingering acoustics of the *dongxiao* and *erxian* phrasing. Both the *nanyin* and the *xiansuo* genre are very old and reflect the cultural acoustics of the Chinese in which true total instrumental interest is the quality treasured but not individual virtuosity in these cases.

THE TANTIAO STRINGS

The fundamental technique of many plucked string instruments is "tantiao". This is a term encompassing the movements of outward "tan" and inward "tiao" on the right hand plucking strings. For each instrument the art of tantiao has been developed to different levels of maturity; the highest forms and the most popular forms are with finger action and the simpler forms with a plectrum. The large non-portable tantiao instruments are the *qin*, the *se*, the *zheng* and others. The portable tantiao instruments are the *ruan*, the *sanxian*, the *pipa*, the *liuqin*, the *hulei* and others. This latter category is also called the "tantiao pipa" strings.

Among the "tantiao pipa" strings, the *sanxian* and the *hulei* do not use frets. The *ruan* was the first classical lute in the world. And the *pipa* was a decendent of the ruan with a new resonator.

The Jiangnan Sizhu orchestra, one of the most popular silk and bamboo orchestras which originated in Jiangsu province, uses a wide range of plucked strings including the *pipa, yueqin,* small *sanxian, zheng, yangqin,* and *qinqin* (or a *zhongruan*). These plucked strings fall into several distinct categories in terms of performance techniques and tone qualities. The *zheng* and the *yangqin* are open-stringed instruments (for the range and tuning

THE *ZHENG* OPEN-STRING ZITHER employs left-hand techniques to achieve nuances and tonal manipulation which are critical to its cultural acoustics.

of the principal plucked strings, refer to Lee, 1979). The *zheng* is performed with fingernails and the *yangqin* is performed with a pair of "Zhu" (bamboo hammers). The *pipa, yueqin, qinqin, ruan, liuqin* and *sanxian* belong to the "Tantiao" system. Their performance techniques are based heavily on the fundamental action of "tan," playing with the index finger to the left or downward, the "tiao," plucking the string with the thumb upward or to the right. *Sanxian* differs from the rest of the members of the "Tantiao" family, especially in left-hand

techniques. It is not a fretted
plucked string and a different
variety of manipulations of the
tone is possible on the *sanxian.*
The plucked strings have a long
history of ensemble cooperation.
Let us look at the traditional
partnership of *pipa* and *sanxian*
in "Tanci" for example.

"Tanci" of the Jiangsu
province is a well-known style
of music in which recitative
singing is accompanied by
instruments. Among the five
principal categories of Chinese
music, ballad singing is the
closest to instrumental music. In
fact, numerous instrumental

PIPA IS POPULAR AS A BALLAD
SINGING INSTRUMENT - for
centuries artists accompany their
own voice with the *pipa.*

music compositions were developed in ballad singing and distilled
into "pure" instrumentals. In the Qing dynasty, the principle
instruments used in "Tanci" was already *sanxian* and *pipa,* with
the occasional addition of *yangqin.* Today, when only one
instrument is used, it is most likely the *sanxian.* When two
instruments are used, the traditional partners *sanxian* and *pipa*
are played by a male performer and a female performer
respectively, the upper part of the melody being performed on
the *sanxian* (small *sanxian*) and the lower part on the *pipa.* In a

joint venture of "Hui Shu," several *pipa*'s, several *sanxian*'s, the *qinqin* and the *erhu* are used.

THE TANTIAO STRINGS - AN INTEGRAL PART OF THE FUNDAMENTAL TANBO ORCHESTRAL SPECTRUM

The second fundamental Chinese orchestral spectrum is "tanboyue", or plucked strings. It is well known that the plucked string orchestra of China is the most complete in the world. It is complete in several ways, but most importantly in the compliments of resonator types, acoustical material and

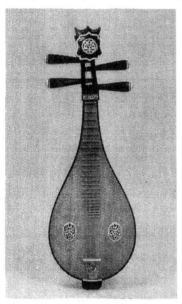

performance techniques. The resonator types and acoustical materials used are not haphazard, but have been developed for orchestral group use over the centuries. On top of that, performance techniques most highly developed allow a vast number of tone patterns to be used by composers of the plucked-string orchestra music. As a result the plucked string orchestral group possesses the powerful capabilities of tonal contrast, dynamic contrast and textural contrast.

THE HIGHEST REGISTER MEMBER OF THE TANBOYUE PLUCKED STRINGS IS THE *LIUQIN*. Plectrums are used to play.

What we are discussing here is the function of plucked strings as a fundamental tonal spectrum for the orchestra. This is a much broader use of this acoustics in concept than what is represented by the plucked string ensemble used in pieces like "Three Six" or "The Camel Bells." In those compositions the plucked strings were treated almost strictly as individual tones to be exploited and as components of a multi-part harmony. Those are simplistic uses. One should look at the breadth of the harmonic content in this fundamental spectrum and treat it as an orchestral texture capable of growing and shrinking.

Let us examine what makes this group so versatile. This branch of the Chinese orchestra is unusually rich in tonal quality. It encompasses:

- *high-frequency range plate resonators excited by tantiao plucked performance,*
- *low-frequency range plate resonator excited by tantiao plucked performance,*
- *middle to low frequency range membrane resonator excited by tantiao plucked performance,*
- *broad frequency range plate/box resonator excited by jixuan struck performance,*
- *low range long resonator/long string open-string excitation, and*
- *low and broad range long resonator/long string fingerboard excitation.*

The extent of spectral versatility of this component is no less than that of the shengguanyue. The combination and organic utilization of both groups are unmatched anywhere.

The more commonly used cooperative spectrum from this group evokes specific musical interest and musical psychology. The high to middle range cooperative spectrum involving the *liuqin* (high-range curved-back plucked lute), the *yangqin* (the grand hammered dulcimer), and the *pipa* (the curve-backed grand lute) spans a range of effects to the audience. It can provide a wide range from cold and dry sound to somewhat heated sound, but the real warmth does not begin to be detected until the *zhongruan* (the mid to low range flat-back round lute) joins in. This is ironical. The *sanxian* (the bass long-stringed membrane-resonator lute), the *zheng* (the open-stringed zither with a large and long resonator providing a broad range of tones from low to high), the *se* (the even-larger open-string zither with a long resonator), and the *daruan* (the bass flat-backed round lute) provide a whole range of powerful low frequency for outlining harmonic or melodic skeleton in compositions, and for mood setting. Strong characters in different ranges can be handled forcefully with the *liuqin* and the *sanxian* when their tones become associated with specific characters. Moving and unstable musical motives are more easily handled with the *qin* (the unique instrument offering five octaves of open-string, full-stopped, and harmonics tones), the *zheng*, and the *se*.

The highest register member of the "tanboyue" plucked strings is the *Liuqin*. This small *pipa* is so high that instead of right-hand fingers, plectrums are used to play. The tantiao family of *pipa*, *liuqin* and other have acoustical radiation on stage of the dipolar type. This means it makes no difference whether they are placed on the left side or the right side of the stage. On the other hand, if they are placed in the middle facing the audience, the effects are the weakest.

REFERENCES

Cao, Anhe, Introduction to Pipa, in *A Collection of Papers on the Study of National Music* (in Chinese), the Music Press, Beijing (1957).

Chang, Ren-xia, in *A Collection of Papers on the Study of National Music* (in Chinese), the Music Press, Beijing (1957).

CMSNA, Exhibition on the Music of the Chinese Orchestra, *Chinese Music*, 3, 60 (1980).

Exhibition on the Music of the Chinese Orchestra, University of Chicago, USA, August 11-12 (1980).

Jia, Weihan, The Origin and Reformation of the Mongolian Plucked String Instrument - Huobusi (in Chinese), *Yueqi* 1981/1 (1981).

Lee, Yuan-yuan, The Liuye-Qin and Wang Huiran, *Chinese Music*, 2/2, 6 (1979).

Ng, Kok Koon, Xiansuo Shisan Tao - A Study (I), *Chinese Music*, 3/2, 42 (1980).

Shen, Sin-yan, Foundations of the Chinese Orchestra, *Chinese Music*, 2, 32 (1979).

Shen, Sin-yan, Foundations of the Chinese Orchestra (2), *Chinese Music*, 3/1, 16 (1980).

Shen, Sin-yan, The Tantiao (Pipa) Strings, *Chinese Music*, 4/1, 3 (1981a).

Shen, Sin-yan, What Makes Chinese Music Chinese? *Chinese Music*, 4/2, 23 (1981b).

Shen, Sin-yan, The Shanghai Traditional Orchestra and He Wu-qi, *Chinese Music,* **5,** 43 (1982).

Shen, Sin-yan, Instruments of the Orchestra, *Chinese Music,* **7,** 31 (1984).

Shen, Sin-yan, On the Acoustical Space of the Chinese Orchestra (in Chinese), *People's Music,* 1989, No. 2, 2 (1989)

Shen, Sin-yan, Pan Gu Creats the Universe - Mao Yuan and the Dance of Yao, *Chinese Music,* **19/**2, 24 (1996a).

Shen, Sinyan, The Music of Peng Xiuwen, *Chinese Music,* **19/**4, 64 (1996b).

Shen, Sin-yan, Yu Liang-mo Plays "Song North of the Border", *Chinese Music,* **21/**2, 35 (1998).

University of California at San Diego Arts & Lectures, Program Notes by Shen Sin-yan for the Silk and Bamboo Ensemble, March 9, 1990 (1990).

Wang, Guangqi, *A History of Chinese Music* (in Chinese), Taiping Book Co., (1962 printing, book written in 1931).

■

Yangqin: the Butterfly Harp

In today's Chinese orchestra, one finds an indispensable plucked string instrument - the *yangqin*. Many have called the *yangqin* the butterfly harp because of its butterfly shape. This is an instrument made of a large flat sound box with dozens of horizontal strings on a trapezoidal butterfly-shaped resonator, and played with a pair of bamboo strikers. The most fascinating thing about this instrument is its power of musical expression beyond other hammered dulcimers. One very recent example can be given here. One summer in the 1970s, during my visit to the Tanglewood music camp of the Boston Symphony, I attended a prelude concert in which three guest musicians from China played solos on their own instruments: *pipa*, *erhu*, and *yangqin* and the players had not been particularly noticed by the audience or the music director of the orchestra, since their appearance was mainly for the purpose of accompanying the *erhu*, the star instrument of the main Chinese concert. In the prelude recital, Huang He, student of Xiang Zu-hua, who is an author of *Chinese Music*, played a piece: "Su Wu Shepherding". This is a *yangqin* solo arranged by Zhao Dian-xue of Liaoning, a province in northeastern China, around 1920. The audience responded to the music with a very warm reception. The music

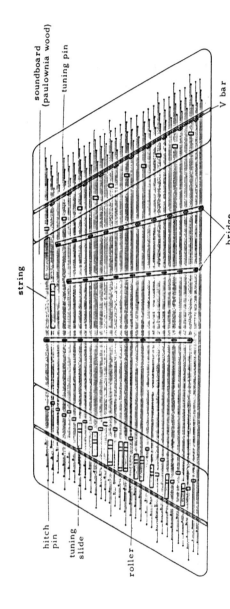

soundboard (paulownia wood)

tuning pin

V bar

bridge

string

hitch pin

tuning slide

roller

TOP VIEW OF THE BUTTERFLY HARP - THE *YANGQIN*. A small version with only three bridges is shown, with strings, hitch pin, tuning slide, and rollers.

director of the Boston Symphony, Seiji Ozawa, also enthused over this instrument, which originally was just another dulcimer to him. He probably did not expect this dulcimer to generate such pristine trains of notes and to have such a *command on the emotions of the audience.* Later in the formal concert on Sunday, Huang He was asked to give an encore after the *erhu* and the *pipa* concerto works which were officially on the program.

THE INDISPENSABLE INSTRUMENT OF THE CHINESE ORCHESTRA

Among the "tantiao" family, the *yangqin* belongs to a subgroup of horizontal instruments whose members include the categories of the *qin*, the *zheng*, the *se* and the *yangqin*. This is in contrast with the lutes which are hand-carried and portable instruments, including the *ruan*, *pipa*, *qinhanzi*, *hulei*, *liuqin* and others (These belong to the subgroup of the vertical members of the "tantiao" family of China (see Shen, 1981 and Shen, 1991). The *yangqin* is both a plucked string, a percussion instrument and a harmonizing instrument. Without the acoustics of the *yangqin*, many types of ensembles or orchestra do not adequately function together. The conductor Zeng Xun once said that the *yangqin* and the mouth organ *sheng* were the indispensable instruments of the Chinese orchestra, and he was quite right.

The *yangqin* is a multi-stringed Chinese dulcimer in which tone is produced by struck strings. Among the non-tantiao plucked strings, the yangqin is a hammered string instrument, played by striking one or two sets of strings with a bamboo striker held by the player and there are two strikers, one in each hand. Perfromers use a pair of elastic bamboo strikers covered with rubber or leather. The vibration of the strings is transmitted to a trapezoidal wooden soundboard by means of bridges over which the strings are stretched. Among the well-known Chinese plucked strings, the *zheng*, the *se* and the *yangqin* are open-string instruments. On these instruments, the open-string pitches (as opposed to a pitch obtained by stopping the string with a finger) comprise the great majority of pitches taking part in music making (For comparison, consider the piano, the open-string pitches comprise a hundred percent of the pitches taking part in music making). Although classified as an open-string instrument, *yangqin* performance requires frequent use of tension-altering or length-altereing manipulations. It is an extremely important member of the Chinese orchestras and is popular in ballad singing accompaniments. The modern *yangqin* has four or five bridges with sets of strings on each bridge pitched whole steps apart and neighboring sets of strings on adjacent bridges pitched a fifth apart, thus allowing a complete chromatic scale to be played in all keys. Its range covers one octave below middle C and two and half octaves above. Yan Lao-lie, Chen De-ju, Yang Jing-ming, Xiang Zu-hua, Lee Yuan-Yuan and others gave the *yangqin* increased importance as a solo instrument. Performing extensively in North America and Europe, Lee Yuan-Yuan has elevated *yangqin* music to new heights internationally and has written a substantial series of research papers and publications on *yangqin* artistry.

Yangqin of four sizes are popular today. The smallest one contains two bridges. On each bridge, there are about ten sets of strings, the range covers three octaves, from E_3 to D_6 (C_4 = central C). The medium sized one has three bridges and its range starts from D_3 to D_6. The large *yangqin* contains four octaves and its range covers from G_2 to G_6. The tuning follows the universal rule of most string instruments. In other words, the notes generated from the right and the left sides of the bridge of the same set of strings different with a fifth. On a small *yangqin*, the note of the string set on the right side of the left bridge is tuned one octave higher than that of its corresponding set on the left side of the neighboring bridge on its right. This will ensure that the small *yangqin* also possesses a large enough compass. In the case of the large and the medium *yangqin*, the tuning is a little bit different from that of the small *yangqin*. The difference allows the playing pattern to be the same for most of the keys. The tuning of a large *yangqin* is shown.

For an instrument with so many strings, tuning could always cause trouble. Small rollers and slides are installed on the medium and the large *yangqin* for the purpose of fast fine-tuning and modulation. This invention was done by Yang Jing-ming who was the *yangqin* player of the Central Broadcasting Chinese Orchestra in Beijing during the fifties.

The *yangqin* is played with the striking movement of a pair of bamboo strikers. Many of the *yangqin* techniques are made possible due to the elasticity of the bamboo. It is this fact that makes the *yangqin* unique among the Chinese plucked strings. As we understand, the Chinese plucked string instruments group is the most developed among the world's plucked strings. For certain plucked string to gain popularity and respect, or even to survive in this family, they must prove to be very good.

The most fundamental technique on the *yangqin* is "tan" or "strike" (see below). Generally, it starts with the left hand or

the right hand followed by the other hand and so forth. The
movement of "striking" on the *yangqin* corresponds to the
"plucking" on the *pipa*, or other plucked strings. If the striking is
done on one or two sets of strings with a speed of at least 680
strokes per minute, then it is called "lun-yin" (輪音 tremolo)
(彡), which is common also on most Chinese plucked strings.
"Tan-lun" (彈輪 tapping) is another basic technique for *yangqin*.
When the striker hits the strings with proper wrist and finger
control, the elasticity of the bamboo will keep the head of the
striker jumping up and down on the strings with the remaining
energy of the first hit to produce a very fast and short tremolo.
Tapping gives a typical *yangqin* effect. It can be done with both
hands (牛) or just the left hand (牛) or the right hand (牛).
In the Si- chuan styled *yangqin* performance, short tan-lun is
expanded to a very long tan-lun. Usually, the long tan-lun is
done with the left hand and is kept going for a whole passage,
when the right striker is playing the melody. A special name
was given to the long tan-lun. It is called - "lang-zhu". With the
same kind of application of elasticity and the energy of the first
strike, but moving the striker up or down from the first hit, one
can generate three to four extra notes in addition to the first note.
It is called down or up "hua-tan" and is illustrated on the next
page. The "yin" on the *zheng* (the 16 or 21 stringed open-string
plucked zither) can also find its appearance in the *yangqin*
techniques. It is called "rou-xian" - the note is raised periodically
by enlarging the tension of the strings. In addition to the above
techniques, staccato, trill, arpeggio, pizzicato, and harmonics, etc.,
are also basic *yangqin* techniques. All of the above are counted

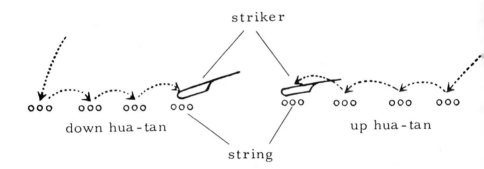

HUA-TAN IS A TYPICAL PERFORMANCE TECHNIQUE ON THE *YANGQIN* accomplished by bouncing on the strings.

as "techniques" and not "embellishment". Embellishment in Chinese is generically used to describe the expansion of a melody.

REGIONAL ORCHESTRAS AND YANGQIN ARTISTRY

Many of the *yangqin* schools are developed on the foundation of regional orchestra, ballad singing, or theatrical music. For example, the Jiang-nan school has its roots in the silk and bamboo school of Jiang-nan in the south of the Yangzi River in Jiangsu province, and Cantonese styled *yangqin* in Cantonese music (a generic term for orchestral music of Guangzhou, Guangdong province). Now the best known *yangqin* schools in China include the Cantonese, Jiang-nan, Si-chuan, Northeastern, and Chao-zhou. Each of them has a whole different repertoire.

Among these famous schools, Cantonese *yangqin* is probably the most well-known and popular. It owns the largest repertorire compared with others. In Cantonese music history,

Yangqin: The Butterfly Harp

Yan Lao-lie (Yan Gong-shang) is the most respected figure. He composed four pieces for *yangqin* around 1910: "Lian-huan-kou", "Dao-chui-lian", "Han-tian-lei", and "Dao-chun-lai". Now these four pieces are considered classics by Cantonese *yangqin* players as well as other *yangqin* players in China. They have been adopted dozens of times by many composers into orchestra works or solos for other instruments.

Cantonese *yangqin* is famous for its fancy embellishment on the melody. People who are not familiar with Cantonese music often consider these embellishments very irregular and being impossible to follow. This could be due to the degree of the complexity of the embellishments and also the abuse of these techniques by some low-classed performers in the thirties and forties. Chen De-ju is the first person who ever dealt with embellishment as used in Cantonese music seriously. In the "Performing Arts of Cantonese *yangqin*", he classified the popular embellishments on Cantonese *yangqin* into several catergories. This classification is very valuable in studying the composition of Cantonese music. The scale used in Cantonese *yangqin* is the same as that of Cantonese music. Its fourth step is 3/4 step above the third and 3/4 step below the fifth. The seventh step behaves the same as the fourth in the Cantonese scale.

The reason why Cantonese *yangqin* obtains the highest reputation in the field probably lies in the popularity of Cantonese music in Guangdong. Cantonese, in general, enjoy music playing very much. Small ensembles can be located almost everywhere. In these ensembles, *yangqin* is among the best loved instruments. It is not difficult at all to find amateur players who

SICHUAN YANGQIN - In today's Chen-du City, ballad singing accompanied by yangqin and other string and percussion instruments is still a very popular entertainment in the teahouses.

can perform the *yangqin* with a high degree of excellence. The popularity of an instrument really serves to prepare the appropriate atmosphere for the development of its music.

Si-chuan is a province near the upper course of the Yangzi River. In Si-chuan, mainly in the area of the City of Chen-du, a type of ballad singing called "Si-chuan Yangqin" attracts many audience in the teahouses. Its key accompanying instrument is the *yangqin*. It is now believed that Si-chuan Yangqin was brought into Si-chuan from Guangdong during the years of Qian-long of the Qing period. Today's Si-chuan Yangqin school was directly derived from ballad singing. Most of the old Si-chuan Yangqin soloists were ballad singers too. Its repertoire coincides with many of the melodies used in ballad singing. Although Si-chuan Yangqin was brought into Si-chuan from

Yangqin: The Butterfly Harp

Guangdong, after years of independent development in Si-chuan, it has departed from its original appearance in both the repertoire and the performing arts. This is due to its long time interaction with the local folk songs, and local theatrical music.

Among the old Si-chuan Yangqin musicians, Li De-chai was a famous one in the forties. He left several pieces: "Jiang-jun-ling", "Nao-tai", and "Nan-jing-gong" which were rearranged by Su Xiu-rong, Li Ke-gui, Li Xiao-yuan, and Xiang Zu-hua and published in "Nine Solo Pieces for the Yangqin" (1958) and "Collection of Solo Pieces for Traditional Instruments - Volume on the Yangqin" (1978). Special techniques, such as the wavy "lang-zhu" and the muffed "men-zhu" are widely used in these pieces.

The silk and bamboo music, south of the Yangzi (Jiangnan), is a noted orchestral music school in China. Its flowing melody, charming orchestration and system of harmony has attracted many an audience. Forty years ago, just like in Guangzhou, small ensembles formed by music lovers gathered very often, and could be found all over Shanghai. These musicians played for themselves and whoever wished to listen. Though they called themselves "music lovers", they were experts indeed in the musical genre. Today there still are several such ensembles and clubs surviving in Shanghai and other cities of nearby provinces. However, most of the graduates of the local music conservatories are no longer familiar with the music at all, since a very large percentage of the coursework in these conservatories has not been geared towards the genuine understanding of, and the appreciation for Chinese music.

Yangqin popularity grew with theatrical music historically. During the Ming and Qing dynasties, ballads flourished and grew, and theatrical art developed to become a main characteristic of that era. Court music, however, declined as folk music grew. In the beginning, *yangqins* were used mostly to accompany ballads and regional operas. It was the leading accompaniment for "Qin Shu" (a broad category of ballad-singing performance). This ballad singing form was popular in Sichuan, Shandong and Guizhou provinces and Guangxi Zhuang Autonomous Region. Many regional operas such as those from the cities of Canton. Chaozhou and Shanghai, and those from the provinces of Hubei, Fujian and Zhejaing use the *yangqin* as accompaniment.

There is a story told of an exiled officer in the Qianlong period of the Qing dynasty (about 1770) who brought a *yangqin* to the remote Sichuan province. He sang ballads with a local partner with the nickname "Zhou the Big Club". In the Daoguang period (1821-1851) Zhou the Big Club came to Chengdu from Chongqing and started a team with a blind man who played *dao-qing* (the progenitor of *zhu-qin*, or bamboo castanets) to accompany his *yangqin*. They named the combination "Yugu Yangqin" (Fishing Drum Yangqin). They later expanded their band by adding a *sanxian, huqin, erhu* and *huaigu*, and substituting a *guban* for the *dao-qing*. They renamed their ballad singing "Dagu Yangqin". In a given performance each of the four or five performers sings as well as plays their respective instruments. Their stories usually come from folk tales or adaptations of traditional operas. With heart-

Yangqin: The Butterfly Harp

"YUEYA WUJING" OR "MOON CRESCENT BEFORE DAWN" illustrates the intricate tonal manipulation that characterize *yangqin* music. *Yangqin* language is thus completely consistent with the requirements of person-to-person communication in the Chinese language.

stirring plots, nice voices and rich timber Dagu Yangqin won great numbers of audiences. Now it is popularly known as "Sichuan Yangqin".

According to an old artist the *yangqin* ballad-singing of present day has not changed much in form and tunes from that of 1880. (It was then called "Yangqin Xi" or the Yangqin opera.) "Sichuan Yangqin" was most popular at that time in Chengdu, the capital of Sichuan province. Before the 1911 Revolution (which overthrew the Qing imperial rule) the Sichuan Yangqin performers entertained mainly in the wealthy houses for special occasions such as holidays, birthday parties, marriages and funerals. After the 1911 Revolution with many high-ranking court officials gone, they went to play in the teahouses for the public in addition to entertaining wealthy people. The well-know *yangqin* artists of that time were Li Liansheng, Li Decai and Yi Dequan, who were accomplished both in vocal style and skill on the instrument.

As in other regional operas, Sichuan Yangqin has roles for *shen* (young male), *dan* (female), *jing* (male role for those short-tempered or righteous characters, with painted faces), *mo* (middle-aged male) and *chou* (clown). The vocal styles fall into two major categories: "da diao" or "fan diao (reversed mode)" and "ye diao" or "zhengdiao (regular mode)". Da diao is of ban-qiang form in formal design (refer to Lee Yuan-Yuan and Shen Sin-Yan's "Brief Notes on Chinese Opera," *Chinese Music,* 2/3, p. 31) "Yue diao" has formal design of tunes-in-a-suite type.

About a dozen *yangqin* solo compositions have remained today. "Jiangjun Ling", "Naotai", "Nanjing Gong", "Da Kaimen", "Xiao Kaimen" and "Mourn the Heaven" are the most well-known. Several of them served as prelude music and some were used as interludes during plays; others were performed at banquets, marriages and funerals; still others were for accompaniment of percussion ensembles. The rhythm is turbulent and powerful. After being refined constantly by *yangqin* players, "Jiangjun Ling" and "Naotai" became major numbers in the *yangqin* repertoire.

In the beginning of the 20th century many regions had developed local forms of music. *yangqin* was adopted as the main instrument of "Cantonese music", "Silk and Bamboo School of Jiangnan" and "Shandong Qin-Shu". Through cultivation by generations of artists, the art of *yangqin* has branched out to form several different schools, all of which have their own repertoires well received by local audiences.

YANGQIN COMPOSITIONS & PERFORMERS

"Cantonese Music" is popular among the people in Guangdong province, Guangxi Zhuang Autonomous Region. Hongkong and Macao who speak Cantonese. It is also popular among Cantonese immigrants overseas. Originally, "Cantonese music" was attached to the Guangdong opera as an interlude. Later, independent renditions were performed during breaks, and finally detached to forma new form of music art. Until a hundred years ago there were no compositions for musical instruments alone. In the 1870s, someone composed the Cantonese pieces "Sanbao Fo", "Dao Chunlian", "Xiao Taohong" and "Yanluo Pinsha". In 1910, Yan Lao-lie, a highly skilled *yangqin* player of the silk and bamboo school of Jiangnan, revised "Dao Chunlian" and "Hantian Lei", two episodes from the ancient "Sanbao Fo", and "Lianhuan Kou" from "Laments of a

Widow". The revised versions, more melodious and livelier, became masterpieces of the silk and bamboo school of Jiangnan.

The first theoretical dissertation on *yangqin* techniques is the book *New Compilation of Cantonese Yangqin* published in 1919. The ten years from 1920 to 1930 saw Cantonese music mature. A group of very excellent pieces such as "Yuda Bajiao" (Rain Falls on the Plantain), "Eniao Yaoshu" (Hungry Bird Shakes the Tree), "Yule Shengping" (Celebrate the Peacetime), "Zouma" (Galloping Horse), "Shuangshenghen" (Double Laments), "Sailong Duojin" (Dragonboat Race) and "Pinghu Qiuyue" (Autumn Moon on the Placid Lake) appeared. Based on traditional techniques the creative artists made the new pieces resonant and smooth with distinctive rhythm, rich in southern Chinese life. Records of these pieces made by the New Moon Company were circulated in great numbers outside Guangdong province. Well-known Cantonese music *yangqin* players Luo Yiyun and Lu Wencheng applied the striker techniques -- long tremolo, repeated use of member of tonic chord in counterpoint with melodic progression, octave doubling, approggiatura and staccato -- to their recorded songs "Dao Chunlian", "Lianhuan Kou" and "Yinhe Hui" (Meeting at the Milkway). Other contributors to Cantonese music *yangqin* development from that period are Yin Zizhong, Chen Junying and Fang Han.

The silk and bamboo music school of Jiangnan, popular in Shanghai and Jiangsu and Zhejiang provinces is an orchestra of string and bamboo instruments, of which *yangqin* is a major part. This form of art, as silk and bamboo music artists recall, appeared as early as the Ming dynasty (1368-1644). In 1899 (near the end of the Qing dynasty) silk and bamboo music players has a grand gathering in Shanghai, the first of its kind in history.

After the 1911 Revolution, silk and bamboo music had large audiences in medium-sized and small cities and towns in Jiangsu and Zhejiang provinces and eventually centered in Shanghai. The most popular pieces known then as the "Eight Classics" are "Lao Sanliu" (the Original Sanliu), "Huanle Ge" (Song of Joy), "Yunqing", "Man Sanliu" (Slow Sanliu), "Man Liuban" (Slow Liuban), and "Sihe Ruyi". Most of the "Eight Classics" were written for the purpose of being performed at marriage and funeral ceremonies, temple fairs and holiday celebrations. Silk and bamboo music is a light, melodious and refined as the landscape along the Yangzi River.

In the beginning of the 20th century, *yangqin* Player Ren Huichu (Li Hongzhang's son-in-law) converted "Lao Sanliu" and "Zhonghua Ling", two silk and bamboo music pieces, into *yangqin* solos, which were then recorded by the Shanghai Baidai Recording Company. His renditions, soft and refined, set a precedent for the early *yangqin* art of silk and bamboo music.

Our good friend Xiang Zuhua studied *yangqin* at early age under Ren Huichu. At his Suzhou home Xiang saw several dozen pieces of delicately made traditional double-seven *yangqins* in the shapes of a butterfly, trapezoid or open book. The top of the instruments was made of Chinese parasol wood and strings of copper wire. The copper taper-shaped tuning peg was turned with a hollow copper hammer. The hole of the peg on the wood wore loose easily. To overcome this defect, Ren Huichu tried to replace the taper-shaped peg with a toothed wheel, an original idea at that time.

In more than Cantonese music, Silk and Bamboo music and Sichuan Yangqin that helped develop a peculiar style and features of the *yangqin*, this instrument took hold in other regions too. In the 1920s, country musician Zhao Dianxue from Gaixian county in Liaoning province applied his skills he had learned playing the *zheng* (the ancient open-string horizontal zither) to *yangqin*, he created new techniques for producing sliding, rolling and shaking sounds. He converted the ancient song "Su Wu Shepherding" to a *yangqin* solo. *Yangqin* is also a compatible accompaniment to "Shandong Qinqu". In "Chaozhou Music" *yangqin* performers make broad use of the techniques of variational embellishment and the unique "Cuiban" (imposing tempo). *yangqin* accompaniment renders "Yulin Xiaoqu" (Ballad singing from Yulin) lively; in their dance music minority peoples in Xinjiang Yugur Autonomous Region, Tibet and Inner Mongolia adapt *yangqin* to their local tastes.

Since 1949 the Chinese government has made great effort to promote teaching research of this art form. Great achievements have been made in instrument renovation and performing techniques. More than forty music schools and conservatories all over the country teach *yangqin* to assure the preservation of this national art.

Renovating the instrument is an important aspect in the development of *yangqin* art. The type of *yangqin* "double-seven-octave" that had been used before 1949 had narrow range, small vocal volume, and was difficult to tune and modulate. Music

YANGQIN (FRONT) AND THE TANBO ORCHESTRAL SPECTRUM of Chinese orchestration. Unlike Western symphonies, the fundamental tonal spectrum of the Chinese orchestra are the "shengguan" reeded winds and "tanbo" the plucked and struck strings - yangqin is the indispensable member of the whole orchestra.

professionals have developed many new models. Some of the successful ones are "bianyin" by Yang Jingming from the Central Broadcasting Chinese Orchestra, "lu-lu" type and "all-lu" movable-bridge type by Zheng Baoheng from the Tianjin Conservatory. The main features of their renovations are an enlarged resonator, of higher volume, better tonal quality and a broader range (having more than four octaves with twelve semitones: F (E) -- a^3 (b^3)). Readjusted arrangement of scales facilitates tuning and modulation. A modifier is added to control the lingering sound. All these renovations are effective in improving the quality of *yangqin* although, no new model is yet entirely ideal. Further research is needed.

Gui Xili invented the "501" large *yangqin* which permits the same "zhu" striking pattern to be employed to a much larger portion of the surface of the *yangqin*. It's an exciting development. The inner acoustical design of the "501", however, has not been modified sufficiently to support e.g. the extra-high notes. This can be accomplished by sound posts (Shen, 1981).

The basic striker techniques of *yangqin* include "dan zhu" (single striker), "qi zhu" (double striker) and "lun zhu" (tremolo). There are variations developed from the three basics. Folk *yangqin* players pay much attention to embellishment of rhythm. Applying striker techniques such as successive bouncing, octave doubling, repeated use of member of the tonic chord in counter point with melodic progression, appoggiatura, long tremolo, tapping, and staccato, a player makes a rendition more colorful, smoother, livelier and of stronger vitality. *Yangqin* is an instrument on which not only fast-changing and springy rhythms

Yangqin: The Butterfly Harp

can be played, but also narrative, slow-moving and light rhythms can be played by using techniques of kneading, sliding and plucking.

For the past 30 years, music schools and conservatories have done a great deal of work in collecting and studying traditional *yangqin* music material among folk musicians, compiling textbooks and creating many new pieces. Two books, *Anthology of Solos of Traditional Folk Music -- yangqin Section* (compiled by the Central Music Conservatory, published by the People's Music Publishing House in 1978) and *Music Works in the 30 Years after the Founding of New China -- Selections of yangqin Works* (published by the Chinese Musicians Association in 1980) have introduced the general development of the work in creating, studying and developing *yangqin* techniques. Peking musicians created a number of *yangqin* concertos including "Romance of the Yanhe River" by Wu Haoyie and Yu Qingzhu.

Newly trained *yangqin* players from schools are making headway. Huang He and Xu Pingxin, two students of Xiang Zuhua, have toured England, the United States, Iraq, Hongkong and West Germany. Their performances received favorable comments. The New York Times remarked that their performance was "flawless" and that they deserved the title of "Champion Players". Hongkong critics commented that their skill was sophisticated and the performance exquisite. Colleagues abroad marvelled at the great progress China had made in the art of *yangqin*. International music circles have made such comments as: This instrument, adapted to Chinese culture and developed by Chinese artists, has a major-second step design on each bridge is very flexible for modulating. The instrument's capability is greatly raised with this design. The bamboo strikers are more flexible and elastic than wood hammer. (Europeans used wood hammers.) After 400 years of exploration and creation by Chinese artists, especially during the past 30 years, the Chinese *yangqin*, imported from Persia through Europeans, has become an important art form in the East.

In the published "Collection of Solo pieces for Traditional Instruments - Volume on *Yangqin*" (Renmin Yinyue Publisher, Beijing, 1978), three Jiang-nan *yangqin* pieces arranged by Xiang Zu-hua were included: "Huan-le-ge" (Song of Joy), "San-liu", and "Xing-Jie" (Processional). Xiang started his learning in Jiang-nan *yangqin* at the age of ten from the authority in the field, Ren Hui-chu during the early forties. Reh Hui-chu, the son-in-law of Li Hong-zhang, was a famous musician of the Jiang-nan silk and bamboo school. He was the first person to transplant the orchestral music of Jiang-nan into *yangqin* solo work. He made the very first recordings of "San-liu" and "Hua-liu" (Bai-dai Recording Company). In Xiang's memory, he was also a big collector of *yangqins*. Xiang Zu-hua later joined the Wu-ping Music Association founded by his father at the city of Suzhou. In 1957, he joined the Shanghai Traditional Orchestra which gathered the best musicians in Shanghai at that time and was the best orchestra in China. In fact, even today, we believe that some of the compositions and recordings of this orchestra during 1955-1964 are still unsurpassed. Zhou Hui is another distinguished Jiang-nan *yangqin* player. He has been a long-time partner of the famous flute player Lu Chun-lin in the Shanghai

Yangqin: The Butterfly Harp

Traditional Orchestra. Unfortunately, except for the recordings made by him and Lu, we do not have too much documentation about him. His arrangement and performance of "Song of Joy" and "Zhonghua Liuban" (Moderately Embellished Six Measure) are rare classics.

"Su Wu Shepherding" was a very popular song in China at least since the twenties. Its background is the story of Su Wu, a diplomat during the time of Emperor Wu (140-87 BC) of the Han period. Su Wu was held by the king of the Huns during his diplomatic mission. The king tried very hard to coerce him to betray the Han court but in vain. Finally, Su Wu was exiled to the area of today's Lake Baikal and worked as a shepherd. After 19 years of imprisonment, he was released on the repeated requests of Han and went home with dignity. Su Wu was a highly respected figure in Chinese history. People admired his courage and his loyalty. The words of this song were written by Weng Zeng-kun (1876-1927), according to Qiao Yu. In 1920, a *yangqin* musician at Gai-xian County, Liao-ning province, adopted the melody and wrote a *yangqin* piece bearing the same name. He applied the northeastern styled method of melody variation and expansion and his own unique performing techniques in this piece. His name was Zhao Dian-xue who was probably the only person from the northeastern *yangqin* school to have his name left in Chinese music history.

Xu Ying recorded "Yueya Wujing" (Moon Crescent before Dawn), a very charming traditional solo work, in the fifties. The musical themes are of northeastern origin. His skillful use of hua-tan, and rou-xian expressions in this piece has made it a *yangqin*

151

classic. The note quality and the superb control shows a deep-rooted musical cultivation on the part of the performer. "Moon Crescent Before Dawn" illustrates the intricate tonal manipulation that characterize *yangqin* music. *Yangqin* language here is inspired by the requirements of person-to-person communication in the Chinese language. Xiang Zuhua's "Su Wu" also illustrates this character:

[1]

Here "rou-xian" manipualtion and the glides (, ,) are clearly illustrated.

"Song of a Border Village" composed by Zhang Xiao-feng is a popular work for the *yangqin* and the Chinese orchestra. The melody is a southwestern one based on the "jue" harmony (of "zhi", "shang", "yu", "jue", and "gong"), and the orchestration is absolutely well done.

The most commonly used model of *yangqin* today is known as the "401" *yangqin* (four bridges). A significantly larger *yangqin*, which has a broad range suitable for large-scale solo compositions, was invented by Gui Xili, and is known as the "501" (five bridges). Other models, such as those made in Shanghai and elsewhere, are not popular.

Yangqin: The Butterfly Harp

THE FUTURE OF THE *YANGQIN*

Traditionally, the *yangqin* was a popular and an excellent accompaniment instrument for voice in ballad singing. It has in the 20th Century also become "the" accompaniment instrument for the *erhu* fiddle. With the *sanxian,* the *pipa,* the *liuqin* and the *ruan* in combined action, the *yangqin* blends the whole group with the shengguan reeds and the huqin fiddles. This is a function no other instrument can substitute. It does it in a way that its sound is almost not heard in the total acoustics, and yet without it the orchestra would not have the right synergistic resonance.

The *yangqin* is one of the most important members of the Jiangnan Sizhu orchestra, one of the most popular silk and bamboo orchestras which originated in the Jiangsu and the Zhejiang Provinces (This orchestra uses a wide range of plucked strings including the *pipa, yueqin,* small *sanxian, zheng, yangqin,* and *qinqin,* or a *zhongruan*). *Yangqin* in Jiangnan Sizhu and Guangdong music (Cantonese music) carries the most intricately ornamented melody and ascertains the harmonic bases of the music. To get a feeling of the kind of sophisticated musical performance we are talking about, one may examine any passage from the highly demanding "Wedding Processional" (Listen to the Silk & Bamboo Ensemble). The octave doubling harmonically important is know as "chen yin", and they are marked with an asterisk in the examples. The performance is highly improvisational; The player reacts to the environment in which he or she plays, in particular to whom he or she is playing with. The degree of ornamentation is a function of time and place and ensemble partner.

The popular "Rain Falls on the Plantains" (Yu Da Bajiao) is a good example of the Guangdong styled role of *yangqin*, when its percussive yet harmonizing effects complement the *gaohu* (Cantonese fiddle), the *hengxiao* (side-blown Cantonese flute), the *xiao* (end-blown flute), and the *pipa* (five-finger strum lute). The orchestrational effect of *yangqin* in Jiangnan Sizhu and Cantonese music are quite similar in their acoustics.

The versatility in the performing techniques of *yangqin*, employing a large number of combinations of wrist and finger actions, and the wide frequency range of four to five octaves, makes *yangqin* an indispensable member of the Chinese orchestra as noted by the famed conductor, Zhen Xun. The hammers of *yangqin* are a pair of specially designed bamboo strikers whose hammering surfaces are covered with thin leather. In addition to harmonizing roles, the *yangqin* is used frequently in solo passages as well. The performance of the *yangqin* can be controlled so that within a passage, certain notes can be made muffed and others crisp and bright. "Fishing Song of the East China Sea" provides the audience with the background to properly appreciate the performing arts of the Chinese orchestra including solo use of the *yangqin*. The "Fishing Song of the East China Sea" created in its listener the broadest range of perception from the most lyrical melodic progression to highly symphonic tonal and dynamic contrast. The use of tonal contrast can be appreciated by examining the beginning passage of the "Fishing Song of the East China Sea". Transparent voice of the *sheng*s without vibrato in displaced registers (Shen, 1980) are echoed by the awakening sound of the large *hai-luo*. This is followed by alternately crisp and muffed sound of the yangqin. We illustrate the use of muffed (ˈ) and crisp and bright sounds by referring the reader to the *yangqin* passage selected from "Fishing Song of the East China Sea" by Ma Shenglong and Gu Guanren, performed by the Shanghai Traditional Orchestra with the maestro He Wu-qi conducting:

In orchestral acoustics, the more commonly used tanbo cooperative spectrum evokes specific musical interest and musical psychology. The high to middle range cooperative spectrum involving the *liuqin* (high-range curved-back plucked lute), the *yangqin* (the grand hammered dulcimer), and the *pipa* (the curve-backed grand lute) spans a range of effects to the audience. It can provide a wide range from cold and dry sound to somewhat heated sound, but the real warmth does not begin to be detected until the *zhongruan* (the mid to low range flat-back round lute) joins in. The *sanxian* (the bass long-stringed membrane-resonator lute), the *zheng* (the open-stringed zither with a large and long resonator providing a broad range of tones from low to high), the *se* (the even-larger open-string zither with a long resonator), and the *daruan* (the bass flat-backed round lute) provide a whole range of powerful low frequency for outlining harmonic or melodic skeleton in compositions, and for mood setting. Strong characters in different ranges can be handled forcefully with the *liuqin* and the *sanxian* when their tones become associated with specific characters. Moving and unstable musical motives are more easily handled with the *qin* (the unique instrument offering five octaves of open-string, full-stopped, and harmonics tones), the *zheng*, and the *se*.

The practice of using the tanbo tonal spectrum as fundamental to the orchestra is reasonably popular, but the practice can certainly be improved several fold. A good example is offered by the use of plucked strings as a fundamental tonal spectrum by Liu Wen-jin in "The Unforgettable Water-Splashing Festival." Several movements of that piece truly show the power of the spectrally versatile tanbo group. Ma Shenglong and Gu Guanren in "Fishing Song of the East China Sea" used this group

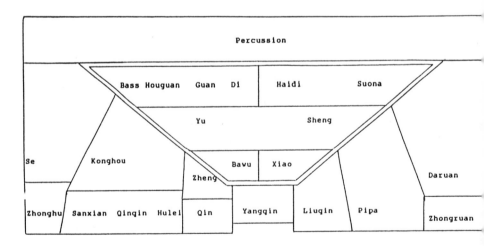

CENTRAL POSITION OF THE *YANGQIN* among "shengguan" reeded winds and "tanbo" plucked strings.

successfully in rhythmic functions as a group. But it can be said that it was a more limited use compared with what this group offers acoustically and in terms of evocable musical psychology.

In the shengguan-tanbo system of orchestra we place the *yangqin*, the *bawu*, and the *xiao* in the front center of the stage. The *bawu* and the *xiao* being directly behind the *yangqin* in the first row of the shengguan group which occupies the center quadrant of the stage, with the percussion directly behind the shengguan group in the same quadrant.

When using characteristic instruments for solo or small group use such as the *zhuihu*, the *jinghu*, the *erhu*, the *banhu*, or the *gaohu* (the acoustical data on the *gaohu* indicates that this is a member of the *huqin* family that is usable in a fundamental tonal spectral group), they can be put in the proximity of the broad-spectral *yangqin*, and the *bawu* or the *xiao*. The *yangqin* thus has the indispensable role as the *sheng* (The *yu* and the *sheng* in modern days are usually all called *sheng* regardless of the number of reeded pipes. Our distinction here for the purpose of orchestration is to put the harmonic usage on the side of the *haidi*, the *suona*, the *liuqin* and the *pipa*, and to put the melodic functions (those of the *yu*) on the side of the *di*, the *guan*, the *zheng* and the *konghou*).

In the grand scheme of instrument, the *yangqin* is silk when instruments are classified according to acoustical material: e.g.

metal: *zhong* (musical bells), *nao* (cymbal), *bo* (cymbal), *yunluo* (gong chime), *daluo* (large gong) stone: *qing*

clay: *xun*

skin: *gu* (drums), *sanxian* (three-stringed long-necked lute) *erhu* (python-skin fiddle), *jinghu* (bamboo fiddle)

silk: *qin* (seven-stringed zither without bridges), *se* (open-stringed zither with bridges), *banhu* (wood fiddle), *erhu, zhuihu, yangqin* (hammered dulcimer), *liuqin* (small lute), *pipa* (pear-shaped grand lute), *ruan* (round lute), *sanxian*

wood: *zhu, wu, gu, ban* (clapper), *muyu* (slit-drum), *qin, se, banhu, erhu, zhuihu, yangqin, liuqin, pipa, ruan, sanxian*

gourd: *sheng, yu* (mouth organs)

bamboo: *xiao* (vertical flute), *di* (transverse flute), *paixiao*

and is plucked when classified according to playing techniques:

wind: *di, xiao, sheng, suona* (shawm), *guan* (cylindrical oboe), *bawu* (flute with single free reed)

percussion: *gu, ban, bo, yunluo, daluo*

plucked: *yangqin, liuqin, pipa, ruan, sanxian, zheng*

bowed: *banhu, erhu, jinghu, zhuihu.*

Yangqin: The Butterfly Harp

REFERENCES

Shen, Sin-yan, Foundations of the Chinese Orchestra (2), *Chinese Music,* 3/1, 16 (1980).

Shen, Sin-yan, The Tantiao (Pipa) Strings, *Chinese Music,* 4/1, 3 (1981).

Shen, Sin-yan, Acoustical Notes on the 501 Yangqin (1981).

Shen, Sin-yan, *Chinese Music and Orchestration: A Primer on Principles and Practice,* Chinese Music Society of North America, Chicago (1991).

■

The True Fiddles of Chinese Music
- A Comprehensive Survey

We now offer a close look at "the prince of Chinese music", the *most popular* string instrument of China. The *erhu* is the *second fiddle*[1] (thus the name *erhu*) of all Chinese orchestras and ensembles, and as a result it is the most popular north and south of the Yangzi River. Our survey covers all instruments related to the *erhu*, the favorite masterpieces associated with them, and their composers. The discussions here will provide the benchmark criteria for any *erhu* music to join the class of "*erhu* classics" that must be torn apart and dissected, in order for future generations to understand what is really involved in *erhu* artistry. They put the *erhu* in proper perspective with respect to its orchestration roles.

The Chinese fiddles have become the best loved and the most intriguing Chinese musical instruments for music lovers in the west today for reasons that can be classified into (A) performance philosophy (B) cultural acoustics (C) musical masters and (D)

---

[1]The *erhu* is second, for example, to the *banhu* wood-plate fiddles in many northern orchestras, second to the *jinghu* (the Peking Opera fiddle) in the Peking Opera orchestra, and is second to the *gaohu* in Cantonese orchestras.

repertoire. When encountering the fiddle (*huqin*) music of China, such as the *gaohu* (high-register vertical fiddle of Canton) music of *gaohu* master Liu Tian-yi, many western violin masters have marveled at their performance freedom. They were comparing, of course, with the performance of the violin, the prince of western instrumental music.

Much of this freedom comes from the philosophy of Chinese music: It is rarely "performed" to entertain an audience. Professor Liu Tian-yi, for instance, can be observed in Yehudi Menuhin's educational films, performing "Niao Tou Lin" (Birds Return to the Woods), in which he was completely absorbed in his fiddle expressions, yet without any facial expression or recognizable body language. This is rare in the west, since music is "performed" in the west ever since the work-for-hire system was in place in the days before Mozart. Musical talents also learn to impress by bodily gestures. This never took place in the Chinese society.

Much of the performance freedom also come from the acoustical construction of the Chinese fiddles, most of which are without fingerboards, thus making it possible to play with both the alteration in the vibrating string length, and the alteration of the tension in the string (Shen, 1990a; Shen, 1990b). The two vibrato techniques are by no means mutually exclusive and they often take place together in a completely integrated fashion in the hands of the fiddle masters. These non-fingerboard fiddles also provide the opportunity for a full contrast of the tones of open string, harmonics, and stopped tones, as required by the compositions.

The cultural acoustics of a music is the specific acoustics (music and sound) which is dictated by the cultural practices governing that particular music making process. The cultural acoustics of Chinese music is a direct result of the many sets of ways of doing things in making music that has come about because of cultural preferences and everyday common musical practices. The choice of tones of musical instruments, the preferred sequence of harmonic intervals, for example, all dictate the cultural acoustics and are a result of the cultural system (Shen, 1981).

Modern studies of Chinese music in the early parts of the 20th century have frequently focused on the court aspect of dynastic Chinese music, and the folk aspect of more recent centuries. Few have gone beyond these more politically motivated angles and truly dealt with the classical philosophies of Chinese music (Shen, 1982a; Shen, 1982c).

We deal here with the true fiddles of China, which are unique in the world. Most bowed strings of the west were transformed from various forms of lute resonators in Medieval times, thus the close linkage between the violin and the *pipa* (the pear-shaped five-finger-roll Chinese vertical lute). All of the Chinese fiddles discussed here were created by musicians as fiddles, for use with a bow, and with a bow only. Pizzicato is thus not very important, nor is double stopping, in their performance techniques.

VERTICAL FIDDLES: THE TRUE FIDDLES

Most Chinese fiddles are vertical fiddles, played on the lap, or between the thighs, with a horizontal bow like in the da gamba, or in the case of the string bass.

The True Fiddles

In this article we present a general survey of the Chinese bowed strings with special emphasis on the *erhu*, one of the most popular musical instruments of the Chinese people.

VERTICAL FIDDLES WITH HORSE-HAIRED BOWS caught the eyes of Marco Polo, as he wrote in his memoir. The *erhu* is the second fiddle of all Chinese orchestras.

There exist more than a hundred string instruments in the family of Chinese musical instruments, most of which are plucked or struck. String instruments were among the very first musical instruments in China for the very reason that the silk industry came very early in the Chinese history (see notes by Shen Sin-yan in University of California, 1990). "*Huqin*" is the generic name for the bowed strings today. The *huqin* family can be classified into two general types based on their physical construction: ones with wooden sounding board and ones with a skin covered resonator (Shen, 1977; Shen, 1979). The ones with a wooden sounding board are generally very bright and the skin-covered ones are mostly mellow in tone. Either type of *huqin* works extremely well with the "tanbo" plucked strings. In contrast with a Western string quartet which consists of all fiddles, the Chinese string quartet has a plucked base. The xiansuo string quartet (see Ng, 1980), for example, uses a *huqin* fiddle (to provide bowed sound), a *zheng* horizontal open-stringed wooden zither and two plucked lutes of different timbre (a *pipa* which is fretted and wooden with a rounded back and the other finger-boarded with a python-skin resonator, the *sanxian*). The spectrum of musical effects resulting from the available timbre and playing techniques provides an endless source of musical interest in such a combination. One of the earliest recorded instruments in the bowed string family is known as *xiqin*, as found in "Yue Shu" (The Book of Music) written in the Song dynasty (960-1279 AD) by Chen Yang. The name *Huqin* was used in "Yuan Shi" (The History of Yuan) of the Yuan dynasty (1280-1368 AD). The most popular *huqin* had many names. To distinguish it from another popular *huqin* of the North which has four strings, known as the *sihu* ("Si" refers to "four"), it started being called *erhu* ("Er" refers to "two" or "second"). Another frequently used name for the *erhu* is *nanhu* ("Nan" refers to "south", where "south" in this context is really "south of Peking") to differentiate between it and the northern style fiddles such as *jinghu* important in Peking Opera, and the *banhu* used in the Clapper Operas (see Liu, 1981). The most important role of the *erhu*, however, is one in orchestration. It is the Second Fiddle, thus *erhu* (Exhibition, 1980; Shen, 1989a; Shen, 1989b).

Almost all *huqin*'s are played vertically. In other words, change of position takes place in a vertical direction. On most *huqin*'s, the horse hair on the bow runs between the strings. Thus, change of string is achieved by fingering actions on the right hand which holds the bow, a situation not accustomed to by most people who are only familiar with the bowing techniques of the violin family.

We will begin with the skin-covered *huqin*'s. The most popular skin here is that of the python. The seven most frequently heard *huqin*'s in this category are: the *gaohu*, the *erhu*, the *zhonghu*, the *dahu*, the *dihu*, the *gehu* and the *bei-ge*.

The *gaohu* is often seen in Cantonese orchestras and other Southern orchestras (see Shen, 1979c; Shen, 1980). It is the brightest of this family and has the smallest round resonator among *huqin* resonators, or a backward-horn shaped resonator. Some *gaohu* have resonators almost as large as the *erhu*, the next instrument in the family as far as size goes, but the resonators are shaped into a horn at the uncovered end so that the "effective acoustical length" is shorter and will therefore have higher resonance frequencies.

The *erhu*, the *zhonghu*, the *dahu* and the *dihu* form the bowed-string basis for Jiangnan Sizhu, the silk and bamboo orchestra south of the Yangzi River. In the Shizhu orchestra, the "Si", or silk section consists of the above mentioned *huqin*'s and a number of plucked strings such as the *pipa*, the *sanxian*, the *zheng* and the *ruan*. The "Zhu," or bamboo section consists of both reeded and unreeded winds, including the *sheng*, a mouth organ, and *di* and *xiao*, the side-blown and end-blown flute families. The *erhu* is traditionally tuned d-a, the *zhonghu* is tuned g-d, a fifth lower than the *erhu*, or a-e, a forth lower than the *erhu*. The *dahu* has open strings an octave lower than the *erhu* and *dihu* an octave lower than the *zhonghu*. The remaining two *huqin*'s in the python skin family are four string instruments: the *gehu*, tuned c-g-d-a and the *bei-ge*, tuned e-a-d-g. The first five in the python family are all without finger-boards, whereas the four string varieties are finger-board instruments. The two families are known as the *erhu* family and the *gehu* family respectively.

Two other popular *huqin*'s in the skin-covered category are the *jinghu*, the soprano fiddle used in Peking Opera, which has a resonator covered with snake skin, and *matouqin*, the alto and bass Mongolian fiddles with trepezoidal resonators covered with sheep skin. There is also the *zhuihu*, principal instrument of "Henan Zhuizi" ballad singing, which is a two-stringed long-necked finger-board instrument having an origin in the *sanxian* (a popular plucked string). The resonator of the *zhuihu* is either python-skin covered or wood-covered.

The class of *huqin*'s with a wooden-sounding board are called *banhu*'s. "Ban" in Chinese refers to wood plate. The three principal types of *banhu*'s are:

(1) **Soprano *Banhu*** - The *banhu*'s are popular in the Bangzi orchestra (clapper opera orchestra) and the Pingju orchestra of Hebei, the Yuju orchestra of Henan, and the Bangzi orchestra of Shangdong. Here Bangzi refers to a specific type of theatrical music popular in the north and the northwest where a clapper (*bangzi* - he lead percussion - clapper - thus the name clapper

opera) is used. The soprano *banhu* is traditionally tuned an octave higher than the *erhu.*

(2) **Alto *Banhu*** - These *banhu*s are tuned a fourth or a fifth lower than the soprano variety. They are the principal instruments in the Qinqiang orchestra of Shaanxi and the Daoqing accompaniment of Northern Shanxi.

(3) **Mezzo-Alto *Banhu*** - These are tuned a minor third or a fourth below the alto *banhu*s. They have a strong low voice and are the popular instrument of the Jinju orchestra and Shangdang Bangzi.

THE *BANHU* IS THE NORTHERN FIRST FIDDLE - this favorite cousin of the *erhu* has been popular since the Tang period.

Chinese Musical Instruments

All *banhu*'s have resonators made from sections of coconut shells covered with a thin sound board of *stescutiaplatonifolia* (tungmu), whose central area is thicher than the edge.

All *huqin*'s, like all string instruments, have their strings stopped at two fixed points. One is, of course, at the bridge. The other stop on the *erhu* family is several turns of string transverse to the strings of the instrument, known as the "qianjin". Whereas on the *banhu* family, it is normally a piece of wedge-shaped wood, known as the "yaoma", or waist-bridge.

Solo repertory for *erhu* presents itself as one of the richest among Chinese musical instruments. Most ancient compositions have been handed down through skilled players (see Minjian Yueqi, 1978), and we normally document the notation of the music together with the name, if known, of the person or persons who handed the music down. Also, just about all classic solo pieces for the *erhu* were made milestones by one or two virtuoso performers. To properly document the music, we also include these virtuosos without whom the music would not have their liveliness today.

All *huqin*'s have an extensive repertory of solo music and a large number of orchestral music in which they each play dominant roles. The *erhu* is the principal accompanying instrument of a number of popular operas south of the Yangzi river, including the Yueju of Shaoxing, Huju of Shanghai and Xiju of Wuxi. In a large number of theatrical applications, the *huqin*'s are used to accompany the human voice. In addition to a purely accompaniment role, the various theatrical orchestras have developed a fairly large repertoire of instrumental music. The well known "Zi Zhu Diao" (Purple Bamboo Melody) is one such piece which evolved in Huju of Shanghai. The music produced on the *erhu* is capable of very high human-like expressions. It can sing and cry. The techniques on the *erhu* is one of the most complex among those of the *huqin* family. Apart from fingering techniques on the left hand for skillfully stopping the strings, the right hand fingering for the proper control of the bow is quite involved. Variations in the tension of the horse-hair plays an important role in the power of expression of *erhu* music. Changing strings on the *erhu* is also achieved principally by right hand fingering techniques. Most *erhu* players find themselves investing the most time in bowing exercises.

For many centuries, *erhu* was not an instrument of the learned class. As a result, very few names were recorded down in history, of *erhu* performers. Zhou Shao-mei, a Virtuoso at the turn of the century, is one of the few names recorded in literatures for the very reason that he was a teacher of Liu Tian-hua, a well known music educator obviously belonging to the learned class. Zhou Shao-mei's favorite "Xun Feng Qu" is still a classic today of the silk and bamboo (Sizhu) school. In "Xun Feng Qu" we find a special style of playing the *erhu* in which separate bowing with Jiangnan styled embellishments add local flavor to the musical expressions. Another musician whose performance was sometimes characterized by this special style is Hua Yan-jun, also known as A Bing. Hua Yan-jun grew up in the community of Daoist monks in Wuxi of Jiangsu Province. The Daoist musicians are well known for their "Sunan Chuida Yue" (Reed and Percussion Music of Southern Jiangsu) and Hua Yan-jun was an exceptionally gifted member of a Daoist orchestra. All we know today about Hua Yan-jun is through the writings of the devoted historians Yang Yin-liu and Li Song-Shou and coworkers. Yang Yin-liu and Cao An-he made recordings of Hua Yan-jun on the *erhu* and the *pipa* in 1950 and the *erhu* pieces "Erquan Yingyue" and "Ting Song" (notated by Chu Shi-zhu and Li Song-Shou) remain at the top of the treasures of *erhu* music today.

Liu Tian-hua (1895-1932), an educator and composer of the May 4th era, was the first to document studies and exercises for the *erhu*. He composed a series of *erhu* and *pipa* pieces, including ten solo pieces of varied styles for the *erhu* among which "Kongshan Niaoyu" (Birds Echo in the Hill), "Bing Zhong Yin" (In Sickness) and "Liang Xiao" (New Year's Eve), for example, are favorite concert programs.

Lu Xiu-tang, an *erhu* artist active during the war years of the forties, composed "Huai Xiang Xing" (Memory of Hometown) and a number of other solo pieces for the *erhu*. His works were widely circulated at the time.

In the fifties, Zhang Shao wrote a series of teaching materials for the *erhu*, stressing traditional technical exercises from theatrical practices including *erhu* exercises for Huju (of Shanghai), Yuju (of Henan) and Qinqiang (of Shaanxi). Zhang Shao's work was pioneering in providing basic study material for traditional *erhu* techniques. Zhang Rui recorded a number of solo pieces for the *erhu* including the Sichuan folk music "Dahe Zhang Shui", arranged by him, that was quite outstanding.

One of the most popular solo work in concerts in the 1960-70s is "Jiang He Shui" (Wailful Wrath of the River), a northern-styled work originally written for the *shuangguan* (a double-reed double pipe). "Jiang He Shui" is originally a popular composition for the wind ensemble with *shuangguan* solo in the northeast (Dongbei). The *erhu* virtuoso Huang Hai-huai very skillfully arranged the piece for *erhu*, and with a *yangqin* (Chinese hammered dulcimer) accompaniment written by Zhang Xing-fu, captured the heart of many an audience in concerts all over. Huang Hai-huai is also the composer of "Sai Ma" (Horse race), one of the very first modern compositions to depict a Mongolian horse race festivity. He himself made the classic recording of "Sai Ma". The most popular recording of "Jiang He Shui" was played by Wu Su-hua.

The *erhu* today is no longer the *nanhu* which only had a southern repertoire. In today's melting pot of performance techniques and musical expressiveness, experiences collected from the *banhu*, the *gaohu*, the *jinghu*, the *zhuihu*, the *zhonghu*, the *gehu* and the *matouqin* are being practiced on every *huqin* in the 20th Century. A large number of techniques from Yuju (Bangzi music of Henan) are now popular on the *erhu*. Two of the *erhu* classics by Liu Wenjin, "Sanmenxia Changxiangqu" (Fantasy on the Sanmen Gorge) and "Yubei Xushiqu" (A Northern Henan Ballad) have liberated Henan styled *erhu* performance from being merely theatrical accompaniment (see Lee, 1979).

Musical styles of bowed-strings in Bangzi (Clapper Opera) music of Shanxi, Shaanxi and Hebei are also popular in *erhu* solo work today. The gracing fingering and rapid-bowing practices of the *Banhu* are now absorbed by *erhu*. "Song of Emancipation" is a good example.

"On the Prairie", a solo composition for the *zhonghu* by Liu Ming-Yuan is probably the first to apply expressions of the *matouqin* on an instrument of the *erhu* family. He met with great success (Shen, 1979b; Shen, 1996). The broad and open tones of prairie music have created new expressions on *huqin*s of the *erhu* family. The trills employing minor third intervals are real treats offered by "On the Prairie". In addition to "On the Prairie', Liu Ming-Yuan also wrote "Mu Ming Gui Lai" (The Return of the Herdsman"), another outstanding work for the *zhonghu*. Liu Ming-Yuan made the first recordings of both works. "Mu Ren Le" (Joy of the Herdsman) by Zhang Xing-lin is another prairie-styled composition (for the *erhu*) employing the La-Mi open strings with a lot of technical complexity and melodic beauty. These works have almost created another school of musical styles for the *erhu* family.

Liu Ming-Yuan, himself a virtuoso on the *banhu* and *zhonghu*, has also arranged a colorful Tibetan composition for *erhu*s in unison titled "Xin Sheng" (New Life).

Other popular recordings of *erhu* music include "Chun Shi" (Spring Poem) by Zhong Yi-Liang, "Zhonghua Liuban" (Moderately Embellished Six Measure - traditional silk and bamboo music), "Qinqiang Zhuti Suixiangqu" (Rhapsody on a Theme from Qinqiang Opera) by Zhao Zhen-xiao and Lu Ri-rong, "Sanchun Bian Liao Yang" (The Mountain Village Gains New Posture) by Zeng Jiaqing and "Gan Ji" (Going to the Fair) also by Zeng Jiaqing.

The cultural acoustics of the *erhu* is present in ever so many compositions for all types of ensembles and orchestras across China. We begin with a survey of this ensemble role, which is quite different from the role of the violin in the West. Whenever possible, we will point out Western equivalents, if they exist.

One of the *erhu* classics for the *tuoyin erhu* is "Guan Shan Yue" (Moon Over the Mountain pass). "Moon Over the Mountain Pass" is composition from the Military music of the Tang period (618-907) for ensemble led by the horizontal flute in Gujue Hengchuiqu. There are two principal ranges for the *erhu* in orchestration: the *zuyin erhu* and the *tuoyin erhu* which are tuned a fourth apart, with the *tuoyin erhu* the lower and mellower version. The silk and bamboo version of "Guan Shan Yue" features the *dongxiao* (the end-blown flute), the *tuoyin erhu*, and the *yangqin* (the hammered dulcimer). Here the performance of the *erhu* is in a silk and bamboo role, frequently providing acoustical support for the *dongxiao*, and serving as lead in alternate movements. The current version was popularized by the Silk & Bamboo Ensemble in North America and Europe.

Another silk and bamboo use of the *erhu* often found in concert programs is in "Xing Jie" (Processional). Here the *erhu* takes charge right from the first upward-gliding D. Padded glissando is used throughout the composition, providing a significant component of the cultural acoustics for the piece. "Processional" is among a large class of ensemble music that has been popular all over China since the 13th century or earlier. It is improvisational within a well-known framework. The *erhu* part has been used as a classical solo piece as well. It is said that, "you never hear the same Processional twice" because every performance is a function of the specific space and time and the human elements present - both musicians and audience.

Padded glissando enables the acoustical effect of a seamless glide. It frequently requires a glissando movement employing three fingers on the left hand simultaneously to achieve the continuous effect. Padded glissando is used in all erhu music, but most frequently in music that has a Shanghai of Jiangnan (south of the Yangzi) silk and bamboo origin. A Bing's fixed position glissando is another frequently used technique to produce the cultural acoustics of the Chinese *erhu*. Such techniques have now been applied to the violin with some success. The fundamental difference between the violin and the *erhu* can not be overcome, however, due to design. The violin, unlike the *erhu*, does not have equally prominent open-string overtones. Thus even with the application of the padded glissando and fixed position glissando, Chinese violin pieces (using the European violin) have not been able to achieve the Chinese cultural acoustics.

In Henan Bantouqu from the ancient central state of Henan, "pre-curtain" music for the popular ballad singing genre is purely instrumental. In "Da Qi Ban" (The Grand Overture), the Silk & Bamboo Ensemble features *banhu* as its lead. Historically this was music composed for prelude before the official performance of ballad singing in historical Henan Province. It had since grown into its own instrumental school. Like the Bantouqu for the horizontal zither the *zheng*, Bantou also feature the *pipa*, and the fiddles. "The Grand Overture" has two prominent fiddle versions, that for the fingerboard *zhuihu*, and that for the free-stringed *banhu*. The *zhuihu* is a versatile long finger-boarded fiddle, with an incredible range and voices. It belongs to the class of *zhuiqin* fiddles whose

THE *ZHUIHU* IS THE FINGERBOARD COUSIN OF THE *ERHU.* Like the *sanxian,* the *zhuihu* uses a long fingerboard. Its repertoire thus favors extremly large glides.

acoustical role has been linked closely to human voice singing in the theatrical setting. The *banhu,* on the other hand, has over the years developed into a school all by itself in Chinese instrumental music. The *banhu* fiddle version of "Da Qi Ban" is quite characteristic of the central state ancient music in the province south of the Yellow River in which almost half of the ancient empires founded their capitals (the other old capital was in Xian). The music expresses warm, uninhibited, happy feelings. It makes extensive use of large position changes and gliding vibrato, all of which are unique of the Henan sub-school of *banhu* instrumental music. These expressions and techniques on the *banhu* are also used on the *erhu*, in such compositions as "Henan Xiaoqu" (A Tune of Henan) and "Yubei Xushiqu" (A Northern Henan Ballad).

"Rain Falls on the Plantain" featuring the *gaohu* is one of the best-known composition from the period of Cantonese instrumental music. As regional as it can be, this music cannot be mistaken as coming from another part of China. The voice of the instrument speaks Cantonese. The intervals are Cantonese: the Cantonese pronunciation has seven to eight inflexions. Accordingly the intervals utilized for *gaohu* performance in classics such as "Rain Falls on the Plantain" has seven, or eight, steps depending on whether the music progresses upward or downward. Delicate instrumentation using the *gaohu* and the *yangqin* ass lead bowed and plucked strings is prominently demonstrated. It abounds with the beauty of Southern China. The lively rhythm and modulation evoke the pattering of raindrops on the plantain leaves as the plantain trees sway in the monsoon.

"Zhonghua Liuban" (Moderately-Embellished Six Measure) features the silk and bamboo *erhu*, using either the *zuyin erhu* or the *tuoyin erhu*. "Zhonghua" literally means "moderately embellished". "Hua" is a frequently used term in Chinese musical aestherics to describe how embellished the acoustics is. The more complex the acoustics the more "hua". There is the saying of "yan hua liao luan" in describing the end result on the audience of simultaneous presentation of too many features where the negative conotation of "hua" is used. The "Liuban" is a class of composition, popular all over China, based on the "Old Six Measure" (Lao Liuban). In this version, the Liuban is moderately embellished and decreased in tempo, making the music highly lyrical and colorful.

The True Fiddles

This piece is technically and musically demanding on the *erhu* and other instruments including the *dongxiao*, the *yangqin*, the *zhonghu* and the *pipa*. Shen Feng-quan and his daughter has a version of the "Moderately-Embellished Six Measure" played on the *zuyin erhu* and the *tuoyin erhu*. It is one of my favorite versions. The Shen version maximizes the use of tonal interest, instead of register contrast popular in Western music. Thus the subtle difference in the tone of the *erhu* (the zuyin version) and the *tuoyin erhu* is used, in addition to register contrast, to generate enormous musical interest. This is done in either a silk and bamboo setting the orchestration of which also employs the other instruments, or in the typically Shen version which uses only the two ranges of the *erhu*.

In all of these cases, the *erhu* acoustics is utilized according to its harmonic characteristics. The *erhu* harmonics are such that it can be picked up among a large number of other tones. When a number of *erhu* is employed at the same time, however, these characteristics would disappear. It would thus be wrong to use many erhu at the same time as a voice, as composers would do in Western music as in chamber ensembles and in symphonies. The *erhu* stands out on a background of violins, however, because of the skin-resonator nature of its construction, and because of the wood plate uniform characteristics of the violin. The same is true when the *erhu* is played against a background of *pipa* and *ruan*, whose acoustics are, once again, based on the wood-plate vibration and are in the lower ranges.

ERHU AND ENSEMBLE MUSIC

It thus becomes clear from the orchestration point of view that there is absolutely on analogy between the ensemble role of the *erhu* and that of the violin. They are completely different acoustically. The cultural acoustics associated with their performance are accordingly in divergence. Too many of the graduates of Chinese conservatories could not understand the theory behind the roles of the silk instruments, and erroneously equated them to Western string instruments in modern-day scoring. The results were disastrous.

A number of ensemble compositions feature roles for the *erhu* and its cousins that have been preserved by the repertoire of the Chinese Music Society of North America (CMSNA)[2].

"Moon Crescent Before Dawn" features a solo *yangqin*. The lead bowed string in this ensemble is the *banhu*. Here the upward glide to "mi" and the downward glide from "la" typify the northern soprano *banhu*. Important intervals are also highlighted such as the large glide "sol-mi" and clean-cut open-string contrast "re-sol-re". These special acoustical effects from performance techniques define the character of the instrument *banhu* in the orchestra. Tension-altering glissando on the *yangqin* are further employed to express inner feelings. The cadences fall on "re", "do", "la", and "sol", not frequently heard in Western music.

---

[2] The Chinese Music Society of North America (CMSNA) was founded in 1969 first as the Chinese Music International Network. It has in the 20th Century preserved the best Chinese music repertory through consistent organized research and performance throughout North America and in Europe and Asia.

"Autumn on the Placid Lake" features the *gaohu.* Lu Wencheng made this Cantonese composition popular in Shanghai in the
first half of the 20th Century. It is the case of a Cantonese musician
writing about the West Lake. It uses incredible embellishments on
the *gaohu* to show the beauty of southern Chinese music. This is a
must-learn for all *gaohu* players. It provides the best training
ground as well as the best display of artistry on the *gaohu* - the
Cantonese first fiddle:

"Song of Emancipation" (Fan Shen Ge) was probably first
written for the *banhu,* capable of leaps in glissando and dynamic
open-string resonance. In a version made popular by Zhang
Xiechen and Wang Guotong, the erhu is employed, and today only
the erhu version is chosen by recording artists in most cases. The
prelude on the *yangqin* and the opening passage on the *erhu* is
swift and lively:

It is so liberated as to be totally unpredictable to the audience. The formal design of "Fan Shen Ge" is however very predictable - one of its weaknesses and the weakness of many 20th Century adaptations of folk pieces. The middle section is highly expressive on the *erhu.* The *erhu* makes maximum use of right-hand long bow techniques. It proceeds via overlapping skeletons of E-A-B-E and A-D-E-A, emphasizing the low E (first finger) with an open string grace note D. The last section is more bouncy on both the melodic progression and the bowing than the first, and concludes with a large downward glissando to C-sharp followed by step progression towards A. The tuning of the *erhu* version does not permit much use of the padded glissando, but all *banhu*-styled glides are prominently utilized. It is one of the few folk pieces that demonstrate the full *erhu* pitch range without any awkwardness.

In discussions of the cultural acoustical effects of erhu performance, I believe the benchmarks are "Erquan" and "Ting Song". "Erquan" (The Moon Mirrored in Erquan) is the best-known modern composition for the *erhu.* It was the product of A Bing (1839-1950)'s life work and thus it is not possible to determine the date of this composition, as A Bing embellished it and further improvised each time he became excited towards the composition in the presence of different listeners. One of those important listener was Li Song-shou who actually introduced A Bing to the musical world. A number of the most important methods of expression on the erhu is to be noted: (1) open-string grace note to decorate the note a whole step above, (2) sudden pause of the bow following a long-bow, ending on a minor third above the main note, (3) fixed position glissando, and (4) bowing control to alter the

relative weights of strong and weak beats. All of these notes pint
to the brilliance of this school of *erhu* performance art. The
cultural acoustics which is very Chinese on most *erhu* performance
has had serious influences from this school.

"Ting Song" (Listen to the Pine) was A Bing's milestone
composition. Not popularly known at first, it has now been
performed several thousand times all over the world by the Silk &
Bamboo Ensemble with a huge following. During the Song Dynasty
(960-1279), Jin U-Zu, commanding general of the Jin army, was
defeated by Yue Fei of the Song Dynasy in a large number of
battles, and had retreated to the Huiquan mountain of Wuxi. He
lay on the large rock known as the "Pine Listening Rock" and
listened nervously to the Song army. Through the musical praise of
the strengths and the integrity of the great pine tree, A Bing's erhu
expresses its admiration for righteousness and patriotism. The
beginning melody presents itself as sturdy boughs of the pine.

rubato

This introduction is played bold as the whistling waves of pine with
unsurpassed confidence and personality. The first and the third
sections surround the middle thematic section, and use *tremolo* in

pianisimo and *detache* to offer a bugle-call melody. The famous middle section begins with *lento poi accelerando* to introduce a melodic progression made up of large leaps in interval in tempo that is ever changing. Continual syncopation provides one high point after another. The *erhu* as the lead instruments in the orchestral version performs separate bowing that is forceful and clear on even the most rapidly moving sixteenth notes.

Having been brought up with the typical sounds of a Western symphony orchestra, many may believe that the acoustics of the violin family is the unique basic source for an orchestral spectrum. This turns out to be entirely untrue. In China, because orchestras were developed over a very long period of time, during which the reeded winds and the silk plucked strings were put into practice in music making by people all over the different parts of China, these groups form the basis for orchestral acoustics. With Chinese orchestras, the fundamental tonal spectrum come from reeded winds (shengguan) and plucked strings (tanbo). And the fiddles play as special color instruments.

The *huqin* vertical fiddles are fabulous solo instruments as we all know, but acoustically they are not the group to be used as a fundamental spectral group. The popular solo *erhu* has an unbelievable penetrating power in the orchestra. They also have their power in a group. But from the angle of orchestral efficiency, the *erhu* group is better accompanied than serving as fundamental tonal spectrum of an orchestra. In a concert hall the ear can tract pitch, tone color and dynamic nuances of instrumental tones with speed and precision. It has been recognized that the ear is most effective with tones consisting of specific harmonic makeup. The ear reacts favorably to the solo *erhu* spectrum but less so to an ensemble *erhu* spectrum. The same is true of the *zhonghu*, the mid-range *erhu*, and the *dahu*, the low-range *huqin*. This phenomenon has to do with the relative strength of the lower partials with respect to the upper, and the pattern in which the upper partials fall off. In terms of orchestral acoustics, the *huqin* (especially the membrane-resonator *huqin*) does not perform in the fundamental tonal spectrum role compared with the solo (or duet) role. On the other hand, the shengguan and the tanbo groups do an outstanding job as orchestral basis as far as the ear is concerned. The same is true of the violin group. The reasons are strictly one of musical psychology that is driven by acoustics. Many years ago Arthur Benade and I had an extensive discussion about this and these were our conclusions.

These considerations have widespread implications. The acoustical angle directly affects the analysis of musical psychology before any cultural filtering enters in. These considerations allow orchestras to be designed with a high benefit-to-cost ratio.

Having said that the *huqin* group did not qualify for a fundamental orchestral spectrum, I must say that the *erhu* group in terms of an *erhu* ensemble (not in an orchestra) has tremendous potential. The format of *erhu* ensemble (in unison or in duet) as in "Wave after Wave of Golden Wheat" (Wang Guotong and Li Xiuqi) has its artistic appeal. The *erhu* group singing the South-of-Yangzi styled passage in "Fishing Song of the East China Sea" (see Shen, 1982b; Shen, 1990c) can never be forgotten. These are examples of excellent use of the erhu group with out subjecting them to the task of orchestral basis. The *erhu* solo in "Longhua

Pagoda" (He Zhanhao) in the most depictive passage is also acoustically valid with a Western orchestral basis.

In the regional orchestras of China, there is usually one first fiddle and one second fiddle. There are sometimes a third and a fourth fiddle as well. The Chinese orchestra does not consist of violins or fiddles as fundamental tonal basis. Overtone characteristics are what separates instruments suitable as fundamental tonal basis for an orchestra to be used in large numbers, from instruments suitable not as orchestrational tonal basis but as single color instrument. In the Chinese orchestral practice through the ages, this has come out loud and clear. The *banhu* is an outstanding solo instrument, and works well with *erhu* as its second fiddle, accompanied by plucked strings. The *erhu* itself is an outstanding solo instrument and works well with wind and plucked accompaniment. But as a group, large numbers of *erhu* together become a poor component of an orchestra. In recent decades, some composers have imitated the practice of the Western symphony orchestra, and used *gaohu* and *erhu* in large groups (e.g. 12 or 24) to establish a bowed string basis. This unfortunately works very poorly. The *erhu* has a drum resonator and is highly individualistic in performance. When it is singing in a background of reeded winds and plucked strings, it carries loud and clear. But when it is used in a larger number, the acoustics is just not there to support a good orchestral tonal spectrum basis. The *gaohu* fiddle, however, behaves a little better in a group, primarily because it is muted and the python skin is under such high tension that the resonator almost does not behave like a membrane drum but like a very hard drum, making it closer to a wooden drum. Instruments with a wood plate vibration such as the *pipa, ruan, qinqin, yangqin* which are all plucked in China are much better acoustically to be used as a group. They work together well in large numbers. They are powerful in dynamic range and they are immediately recognized by the music psychology of the audience to serve as a "sound of the orchestra". The *erhu* group simply does not do that acoustically or music-psychologically when there are other instruments present.

SPECIAL COLOR FIDDLES FOR THE ORCHESTRA

The erhu and its cousins are outstanding special color or solo instruments for orchestral and ensemble pieces. The most common special-color fiddles are:

Zuyin Erhu and Tuoyin Erhu

The *erhu* is the universal second fiddle, popular both north and south of the Yangzi River. It comes in two ranges: the *zuyin erhu* and the *tuoyin erhu*. The *zuyin erhu* is tunes c-g or d-a, and the *tuoyin erhu* a fourth lower. The characteristic sound of the *erhu* comes from its "drum" resonator. The open string resonances are most dominant - the choice of register in performance is thus critical.

Banhu

The favorite cousin of the *erhu* is the *banhu* - a wood plate fiddle quite unlike the erhu. The *banhu* family has been popular since the Tang dynasty. It is in fact more historic than the *erhu* but was called different names at different times - among them *xiqin* and *jiqin*. The *banhu* differs from the *erhu* in acoustics as it uses wood plate vibration (The *erhu* uses python skin on a drum resonator).

Zhuiqin and Zhuihu

The more regional cousins *zhuiqin* and *zhuihu* are popular in the Henan and the Shandong areas. These cousins are fingerboard instruments (As you will recall the *erhu* and the *banhu* do not use fingerboards). They both have long fingerboards like that of the *sanxian*, and thus facilitate large-interval glissandos.

Erxian and Gaohu

The *erxian* was the principal fiddle of the Cantonese orchestra. Today it has for most practical purposes been replaced by the *gaohu*.

REFERENCES

Exhibition on the Music of the Chinese Orchestra, University of Chicago, USA, August 11-12 (1980).

Lee, Yuan-yuan, Fantasy on the Sanmen Gorge, *Chinese Music*, 2/2, 23 (1979).

Liu, Ming-yuan, Banhu, *Chinese Music*, 4/2, 28 (1981).

Minjian Yueqi Chuantong Duzouqu Xuanji (Traditional Solo Pieces for Chinese Instruments), Volume on *Erhu* and *Banhu*, Renmin Yinyue Chuban She (The People's Music Press) (1978).

Ng, Kok Koon, Xiansuo Shisan Tao - A Study (I), *Chinese Music*, 3/2, 42 (1980).

Shen, Sin-yan, The Application of Bowed Strings in Chinese Music, *Music and Audiophile*, No. 46 (March 20, 1977).

Shen, Sin-yan, Erhu, *Chinese Music*, 2/1, 2 (1979a).

Shen, Sin-yan, The Music of Liu Ming-yuan, *Chinese Music*, 2/2, 3 (1979b).

Shen, Sin-yan, Foundations of the Chinese Orchestra, *Chinese Music*, 2, 32 (1979c).

Shen, Sin-yan, Foundations of the Chinese Orchestra II, *Chinese Music*, 3, 16 (1980).

Shen, Sin-yan, What Makes Chinese Music Chinese? *Chinese Music*, 4/2, 23 (1981).

Shen, Sin-yan, Zhongguo Yinyuejie Dui Renlei Yingfu De Zeren (in Chinese), *Lianhe Yinyue*, February, 1982, United Music Academy, Hong Kong (1982a).

Shen, Sin-yan, The Shanghai Traditional Orchestra and He Wu-qi, *Chinese Music*, 5, 43 (1982b).

Shen, Sin-yan, Zhongguo Yinyuejie Dui Renlei Ying Fu De Zeren (in Chinese), *Zhongguo Yinyue*, 1982, No. 2, 18 (1982c).

Shen, Sin-yan, On the Acoustical Space of the Chinese Orchestra (in Chinese), *People's Music*, 1989, No. 2, 2 (1989a).

Shen, Sin-yan, On the Acoustical Space of the Chinese Orchestra (in Chinese), *People's Music*, 1989, No. 2, 2 (1989b).

Shen, Sin-yan, On the System of Chinese Fiddles I, *Chinese Music*, 13, 24 (1990a).

Shen, Sin-yan, On the System of Chinese Fiddles II, *Chinese Music*, 13, 44 (1990b).

Shen, Sin-yan, "Fishing Song of the East China Sea"-Review of a Recent Performance, *Chinese Music*, 13, 4 (1990c).

University of California at San Diego Arts & Lectures, Program Notes by Shen Sin-yan for the Silk and Bamboo Ensemble, March 9, 1990 (1990).

Shen, Sin-yan, Chinese Music's First Cover Personality: Liu Ming-Yuan, *Chinese Music,* **19**, 7 (1996).

Chinese Musical Instruments

■

INDEX

CHINESE MUSIC MONOGRAPH SERIES

ISSN: 1071-5649

Series Editors:
Yuan-Yuan Lee Ph.D.
Sin-yan Shen Ph.D.

- CHINESE MUSIC AND ORCHESTRATION:
  a Primer on Principles and Practice

- CHINESE MUSICAL INSTRUMENTS

- CHINA: *A Journey into Its Musical Art*

- WHAT MAKES CHINESE MUSIC CHINESE?

- MUSICIANS OF CHINESE MUSIC

- THE REGIONAL MUSIC OF CHINA

ORDER FORM

(ISBN: 1-880464-00-4)

Chinese Music and
Orchestration   *$17.95*

A Primer on Principles and Practice
by Sinyan Shen

This is a book for any person who is interested in music and culture. It belongs to the *Chinese Music Monograph Series*, the first comprehensive and easy-to-read series on Chinese music. Other titles include: Instruments & Performing Arts, Musicians, What Makes Chinese Music Chinese, the Zenghou Yi (5th Century BC) Music Treasure.

Please print

Name_____

Street_____

_____
                                          Zip
City_____State_____Code_____

Country _____

☐ U.S. US$ 17.95 + shipping/Handling US$3.50

☐ Foreign US$ 17.95 + shipping/Handling US$4.50

METHOD OF PAYMENT (Check one only)
☐ Check or Money Order. (Kindly remit in US funds and make check payable to the Chinese Music Society.) or
Credit Card: ☐ VISA ☐ MasterCard
          ☐ Discover ☐ American Express

Credit   Exp.
Card No:_____Date:_____/_____

Signature_____Tel:_____/_____

Name on
the Card:_____

■ Send to your **usual supplier** or to **Chinese Music Society**, Subscription Dept, PO Box 5275, Woodridge, IL 60517-0275 USA. Tel: 630-910-1551 FAX: 630-910-1561 ■ www:ChineseMusic.net

CHINESE Music

International Journal
ISSN 0192-3749

Your source of timely information - a total solution to your resource needs on the music and culture of the Chinese People and China. *Chinese Music* (ISSN 0192-3749) quarterly covers all phases of scholarly and performance activities in Chinese music and culture. It is the international and English-language forum for original papers concerned with aesthetics, musicology, musical life, performance, the music-making process, composition, cultural acoustics, analysis, orchestration, musicians, global interactions, intercultural studies, dance and theatrical music, and musical instruments. It also publishes news items of importance to the music community and the general public, as well as book and recording reviews.

Indexed and abstracted in *The Music Index*, the *RILM*, the *MLA Index* and by international abstracting and indexing services worldwide.

Chinese Music is the only journal in the world devoted wholly to the study of the music and acoustics of China and the Chinese people, and their relationship to the music of the world.